A Sense of the Sea

Our View of the Sea and How We Got It

Published in the United States by Booklocker.com, Inc., Port Charlotte, FL.

Printed in the United States of America on acid-free paper.

2011
First Edition

Author's biography: www.oeatech.com/consultants/consultant-3/

ISBN Softcover 978-1-61434-538-1
ISBN Hardcover 978-1-61434-537-4

1. Nature   2. Oceanography

In part, we owe our freedom to all who serve the navies of war, but this book is dedicated to my father in particular, who served in the Royal Navy during World War II and the Royal Canadian Navy during the Cold War.

Acknowledgements

I wrote *A Sense of the Sea* with the support of family and the assistance of professionals. Diane, Christiane and Edward, my wife and two children, often encourage me to write. My understanding of the ocean intelligence sector benefited from interactions with U.S. and Canadian marine environmental security specialists. Fond memories of Peter J. Wangersky, my mentor in oceanography, surfaced while writing the first draft. Sharon Lindenburger, my editor, rescued me from the vortex of the draft manuscript, and Frances Robinson generated the book's index. I also sincerely appreciate assistance provided by Katherine Alexander (The Royal Hospital School, UK); Chris Fogarty (Environment Canada); Jacob Hamblin (Oregon State University, USA); Linda Lear (Rachel Carson biographer, USA); Eric L. Mills (Dalhousie University, Canada); Walter Munk (Scripps Institution of Oceanography, USA); Mike Overton (HMS *London* Association, UK); Jennifer Ramarui (The Oceanography Society, USA); and Andy Thomas (University of Maine, USA). Valery Hill, Kathleen Trenholm, and various siblings provided constructive reviews, and Florence Whitehouse (my mother) and Auntie Vera provided rare insight into my father's childhood and naval experiences.

Although odd at the time, I also thank Roddy and Sue for giving me a dictionary as a wedding present. Yes, I am still plogging <sic> along.

Table of Contents

A Sense of the Sea

Our View of the Sea and How We Got It

Brian Whitehouse

Foreword by Walter Munk

Booklocker.com, Inc., 2011
Port Charlotte, FL

Foreword

This volume offers Brian Whitehouse's very personal relation to the oceans. Under the influence of his Navy father and a Dalhousie University PhD in Oceanography, Whitehouse developed a keen interest in what was learned about the oceans during and following WWII, and the people who did the work. This was the era when remote sensing from satellites revolutionized the way we monitored the global oceans. Whitehouse's first use of spaceborne sensors to solve coastal habitat issues occurred during this period. This experience was followed by ten years with the Alliance for Marine Remote Sensing. The reader will find some topics of special interest.

Walter Munk
Secretary of the Navy Chair in Oceanography
Scripps Institution of Oceanography

Preface

Your sense of the sea is as valid as the next, regardless of your knowledge of it.

We all have a sense of the sea, regardless of where we live. But it is possible to sense something without understanding it. I see my car almost every day, for example, but I cannot tell you how an electronic fuel-injection system works. This is why I wrote *A Sense of the Sea*. I sense the common view of the sea is like my view of four-cylinder engines.

We need to know how an ocean works. Our survival depends upon it. I grew up with Rachel Carson's view, in which air, land, sea, and the human race are inter-related components of a single entity, sort of like an engine—except Carson used the scientific term—*ecosystem*. She inspired me. She showed us the 1950 version of how an ocean works. But like other people she also influenced our perception of the sea. Every time you read, watch, or listen to someone else's view of the sea, it influences how you perceive the marine environment. Eventually, your view becomes an amalgamation of such influences, with the result that there are countless views of the sea. It is conceivable for two people to have almost identical knowledge of the sea, but it is unlikely that two people have identical *perceptions* of it. Your knowledge of the sea can be incomplete but not your perception. Your sense of the sea is as valid as the next, regardless of your knowledge of it.

Knowledge and perception are like yin and yang in that they go hand in hand. This is what I discovered as I wrote the book. I have two views of the sea, not one. I perceive the sea as a result of personal experiences and influences of mass-media, and I have knowledge of it as a result of having a degree in oceanography and twenty-odd years of experience studying the dynamics of the marine environment. In *A Sense of the Sea* I present both views. By the time you finish reading it, you will also have two views, assuming you do not already. I spent years synthesizing knowledge presented in section one of the book, but the most rewarding aspect of this adventure was realizing who and what influenced my perception of the sea and how they did it. I present this in section two. You do not need to research anything to reap this reward. Just replace my experiences with yours.

Finally, as additional guidance I present two points of caution. First, in section one I present knowledge of the sea that is based on scientific discovery, to help you realize how the sea influences your life and vice versa. But this is not a science or history text. It is a book about the marine environment. Secondly, if not for World War II, the Cold War and superpowers, I believe our present view of the sea would not exist as such. This may come across in the book as a positive view of war, which is unintentional. Any positive light reflects personal influences of my father, who served in two navies. More than anyone, he gave me my view of the sea. I speculate that within every perception of the sea there exists such a founding influence, whether it be a family member, someone else, or something else. Read *A Sense of the Sea* to discover the origins of your view and to understand the dynamics of the sea that surrounds you.

Introduction:

The Seven Seas

What we see when we think of the sea is a network of ill-defined environments.

The common view of the sea is not based on facts. To convince yourself of this, ask anyone how many oceans or seas there are. Alternatively, ask him or her to name the seven seas, or simply to tell you the definition of a sea. Even seasoned sailors cannot answer these basic queries with confidence, and for good reason.

Oceanography is the study of the dynamics of the marine environment. In other words, oceanographers try to figure out what makes the ocean tick. Everyone knows a few facts about the sea, but unlike other subjects of nature, oceanography is not a prominent subject in public school. My echo boomer daughter had the option of taking it in high school; however, it is not recommended for university preparation.[1] There are undergraduate courses in oceanography, but usually it is studied within elite graduate schools. This means that while most people have seen the sea, either in person or through the views of others, very few understand how it functions. As a result, your understanding of the sea is probably based on perception, not fact. Most baby boomers obtained their view of the sea through personal experiences, mass media, and twentieth-century

---

[1] Baby boomers were born during the post-war period of 1946 to 1964. The Y generation, born between 1978 and 1995, are also referred to as echo boomers.

celebrities such as Jacques Cousteau. His books, films, and television programs captured our imagination and showed us the wonders of the seven seas, but they did not expand our understanding of the dynamics of the sea. They didn't even teach us how many oceans there are or the names of the so-called seven seas.

The reason why no one names the seven seas is that they no longer exist as such. The phrase predates Christ and refers to the bodies of water that comprise Earth's marine environment. Definition of the original seven changed with empire and location, and the phrase waned when explorers discovered and named many new bodies of water. But in 1896, the poet Rudyard Kipling brought the phrase back into vogue when he published a collection of works by the same name.

In his 1957 five hundred and twelve page treatise on the seven seas, Peter Freuchen refers to Rudyard Kipling's resurrection of the phrase "seven seas" as "a triumph of poetry over reality."[2] Freuchen lists the original seven as the Mediterranean, Red, China, West African, East African, Indian Ocean and Persian Gulf, but states that as a result of Kipling they were rebranded as the Arctic, Antarctic, North Atlantic, South Atlantic, North Pacific, South Pacific, and Indian.

As there is no longer a definitive set of the now poetic seven, and no universally accepted definition of a sea, Freuchen's view is as plausible as the next. Wikipedia states there are more than one hundred seas, but in my opinion there is no set number. One reference's gulf or bay is another's sea or collection of seas. Certain references identify bodies of water as seas, even though they are freshwater lakes. Some seas have more than one name, and a subcomponent of a sea may have its own sea name in certain references but not others. In an ad hoc exercise akin to finding Waldo,

---

[2] Peter Freuchen, *Book of the Seven Seas* (New York: Julian Messner, 1957), 33.

on late twentieth century maps I found seventy-five bodies of saltwater whose name includes the word Sea: Adriatic, Aegean, Alboran, Amundsen, Andaman, Arabian, Arafura, Aral, Aru, Azov, Banda, Balearic, Bali, Baltic, Barents, Beaufort, Bellingshausen, Bering, Bismarck, Black, Bohol, Caribbean, Caspian, Celebes, Celtic, Ceram, Chukchi, Coral, Cosmonaut, Crete, East China, Dead, Flores, Greenland, Halmahera, Iceland, Ionian, Irish, Japan, Java, Kara, Labrador, Laccadive, Laptev, Ligurian, Lincoln, Marmara, Mediterranean, Mindanao, Mirtoan, Molucca, Natuna, Norwegian, North, Okhotsk, Philippine, Red, Ross, Sargasso, Savu, Scotia, Siberian, Sibuyan, Solomon, South China, Sulu, Tasman, Timor, Tyrrhenian, Visayan, Wadden, Wandel, Weddell, White, and Yellow. No single reference includes all seventy five and this list does not include known seas whose names no longer appear on these maps, such as the Vermilion Sea and Sea of Cortez off of the Baja Peninsula. Also, as an oceanographer I could not bring myself to exclude the Sargasso Sea, even though its name did not appear on these maps. On the other hand, certain publications refer to the Great Lakes as seas whereas I do not.

The five oceans of Earth are the Atlantic, Pacific, Indian, Arctic and Southern. Many baby boomers likely perceive the planet as having four oceans–the Arctic, Atlantic, Pacific and Indian. The four oceans view considers the Southern Ocean to be the southern parts of the Atlantic, Indian, and Pacific Ocean. The five oceans view is similar to Peter Freuchen's definition of the seven seas, except he divides both the Atlantic Ocean and Pacific Ocean into two, and calls the Southern Ocean by its other name–Antarctic Ocean.

Somehow, when growing up I remember a Southern or Antarctic Ocean, even though the name Southern Ocean did not come into vogue for me until the last quarter of the twentieth century, in association with around-the-world yacht races and satellite images of diminishing polar ice formations. Both my enlightenment and confusion originated with Rachel Carson. Her 1951 epic book, *The*

Sea Around Us, talks about both an Antarctic and Southern Ocean, but Rachel Carson also refers to the Arctic as both a sea and an ocean. In which case, did she believe we had four oceans or five? Carson was an acclaimed marine naturalist with a strong background in science, yet even she seemed ambiguous about the number of seas and oceans and their names.

This uncertainty in the number of oceans and their nomenclature may originate with the International Hydrographic Organization. It included the Southern Ocean in the 1937 edition of its *Limits of Oceans and Seas* publication, but excluded it from the current edition, which dates from 1953. Then, in 2000, the Organization declared the region to be the Southern Ocean again while not releasing an updated version of its official publication, which is recognized internationally.

The 2005 edition of the National Geographic Society's renowned world atlas, the current edition as I write, maintains this four-ocean view, five years after the International Hydrographic Organization decided to recognize the Southern Ocean again, but not officially. First recognition of the Southern Ocean in a National Geographic sponsored atlas that I could lay my hands on occurs in *Ocean–An Illustrated Atlas*, published in 2009. Yet, even in this recent publication, a map that spans the inside back cover identifies the Southern Ocean with the qualification "A Fifth Ocean?" This map also refers to it as the Antarctic Ocean and Austral Ocean and states that there is no international agreement on this subject.

I am uncertain as to who holds the responsibility for establishing and promoting the definition of a sea or ocean, or other such facts, but I believe the public fills this knowledge void with perceptions founded upon popular opinion, folklore, regional politics, and the views of the rare individual who attracts the attention and respect of the masses. We do not live in the sea and do not study it in public school; thus most people do not gain knowledge of it firsthand or formally.

Based on personal experience and what we see on television and silver screen, or read in novels and newspapers, we form land-based perceptions of the sea around us. What we see when we think of the sea is a network of ill-defined environments. Without official definition, your view is as correct as the next. For a recent example, news headlines from the west coast of North America for the month of November 2009 suggest we now have a new sea–The Salish Sea. It washes the shores of both the United States and Canada and comprises the waters of the Straits of Georgia and Juan De Fuca, Washington State's Puget Sound, and waters in between. Newspapers from the region lead us to believe this discovery arose as a result of our knowledge of marine biology. A respected biologist coined the name on the grounds that this person viewed these waters as an ecological entity. Is this the new definition of a sea–an ecosystem? Whether you view these western bodies of seawater as an ecosystem depends upon your perspectives of time and space. You could, for example, view them not as one ecosystem but as a multitude of nested ecosystems. In which case, why not define these waters as a collection of seas?

I am being cynical here, and the referenced biologist's rationale is not an isolated point of view. Managing the sea as an ecosystem is sound and accepted advice. This was not always the case, and in my view, Rachel Carson first presented it to the general public in the 1950s. My point is that this new sea is a result of popular opinion and political correctness, not definition. The lands that border these waters were first populated by aboriginal Coast Salish nations. The name Salish Sea recognizes their heritage a few thousand years after they got there. Given that the Coast Salish people themselves do not refer to these waters as the Salish Sea, but as Sqelatses, khWuhlch, Whulge or Whulj, the name satisfies language requirements of more recent settlers.

Like our perception of the seven seas, language evolves. Today, when we say that someone is at sea or he or she is sailing the seven seas or the ocean blue, it simply means the person is somewhere within the marine environment, whether it be on one of the five oceans or numerous seas. As a sailor, I take the simple view that if it is saltwater, then I am at sea, and if it is brackish, then I soon will be, assuming I am not sailing on one of those bizarre inland saltwater lakes. When referring to the marine environment in general, people often use the words "sea" and "ocean" interchangeably.

It is not that we lost a sea or ocean or found another sometime during the twentieth century. Although Antarctica is a dynamic region, it did not morph into something completely new over a period of years to a few decades. It is our *perception* of the sea that changed during this period and it continues to do so, and I am not only referring to those who sail the seas for a living.

Eight of the world's ten largest cities are located by an ocean. In 2008, approximately fifty percent of the human population, more than three billion people, lived within one hundred kilometers of the sea, including fifty-three percent of Americans.[3] Four hundred million Chinese live by the sea, which is more than ten times the population of Canada.

A geographically disproportionate number of people live in the coastal zone. In the United States, for example, the coastal zone represents eleven percent of that country's area but houses more than half its population. Canada, by comparison, is an anomaly in that although it is washed by three oceans, the majority of its population does not live by one. Regardless, the sea is no longer just about food, transportation and warfare, as it once was. It holds ninety-seven percent of the planet's water. Geographically, it divides nations, but environmentally it unites them. Even those who do not live by the sea feel the influence of its global effects because the sea impacts the daily priorities of all living creatures: security, a constant demand for energy, and quality of life. Yet, unless you are an oceanographer or

---

[3] *UN Atlas of the Oceans*, http://www.oceansatlas.org/.

addicted to nature programs shown on public television, you likely have cursory knowledge of what makes the ocean tick. Even consensus on how to name them eludes us, with the result that a poet is as likely as anyone to influence our view of the sea, and there is much more to this issue than merely names. We have yet, for example, to quantify the oceans' role in climate change.

Understanding what makes an ocean function is as much about change detection as about observing its features. When scientists study not only the composition of the sea but also its dynamics–how it varies in time and space–they are viewing it from the perspective of an oceanographer. The subject of oceanography applies the basic sciences of biology, chemistry, geology, and physics to the sea. This is why oceanography is not an integral component of public school or undergraduate curricula. Prior to studying oceanography it is best to first learn the basics of science. This is why I found myself at the right place at the right time when I stepped aboard a coast guard vessel in the late 1970s, with a bachelor of science degree in hand. I knew almost nothing about oceanography, but I had just devoted four years of my life to studying the basics of science. My father did not advise me to major in science and I had no idea what I wanted to be when I enrolled in university. I simply followed the path that lay before me. In the 1960s and 70s, science was held in high esteem and it was not uncommon to see scientists featured on the cover of magazines such as *Time*. Not so much now, as you are just as likely to have a politician or editor slam the science community as praise it, especially when it comes to the environment. It was not like that when I was growing up.

Once I started to sail the seas, I realized the need for a graduate degree in order to become a professional oceanographer. There is a maxim that ninety percent of the advancements in science are made by ten percent of the world's scientists. If true, this means that the majority of scientists are like Slartibartfast in *The Hitchhiker's Guide to the Galaxy*, painstakingly devoting their professional lives to the crinkly edges of their profession. I obtained a PhD in oceanography, specializing in chemical oceanography, but quickly came to the conclusion that I was not among that ten percent of elite scientists. In hindsight, I may have been hasty for I have since come round to Frederick Hunt's view of the subject.

As a Harvard professor specializing in acoustics in the 1950s, Hunt believed that great inventions are not "an isolated act of creative imagination on the part of a single individual." [4] Instead, the state of a given field percolates along until remarkable invention is produced at the hands of one person or another. Like a lottery for the enlightened, there is an overall winner, but as Hunt observed, there are many others who almost had it right.

As an example, Hunt references Alexander Graham Bell's discovery of the telephone–the most valuable patent ever issued, according to Hunt. The significance of this example is that Elisha Gray filed with the United States Patent Office with regard to telephony on the same day as Bell, 14 February 1876, but a few hours later and his filing included intent to file a more complete description thereafter as a component of a formal patent application. [5] Meanwhile, Bell's complete application proceeded to patent. Gray was one of several who claimed to have developed the telephone during this period. In each case, Bell successfully defended his claim.

Frederick Hunt's logic also demonstrates that major advancements in a given field of science or engineering often occur over relatively short periods of time. With respect to the field of transducers and electroacoustics, in addition to Bell discovering the telephone in the 1870s, Edison discovered the light bulb and phonograph, and Rayleigh published his *Theory of Sound*. The first few years of the 1880s were almost as productive.

---

[4] Frederick V. Hunt, *Electroacoustics: The Analysis of Transduction and its Historical Background* (New York: John Wiley & Sons, 1954), 23.
[5] Ibid., 31.

Like life itself, great discovery in a given field is nonlinear. Thus the saying about being in the right place at the right time. The reverse of this is that you can, through no fault of your own, be in the right career at the wrong time. This is why, unlike my parents and others of their generation, I do not ask my university daughter what jobs are available in her chosen profession. By the time she graduates the answer will likely have changed. As my father discovered through his career choices, you can position your view such that you will not be at the center of great innovation even if you have the ability to excel. But again, getting it right is akin to winning the lottery.

Alas, on the rare occasion that I read for pleasure in my youth I chose adventure novels over treatises on electroacoustics by Harvard university professors such as Frederick Hunt. Thus, I did not benefit from his wisdom until much later in life, and although Slartibartfast of the aforementioned *Hitchhiker's Guide* won an award for the fjords of Norway, I did not want to become a character in a Douglas Adams novel. Instead, I left academia to pursue a career in applied oceanography. As oceanography is itself an applied science, the term applied oceanography is redundant. It means I apply oceanographic knowledge to everyday life.

As it turned out, although the 1970s produced defining moments that changed our view of the sea, I have a different perception of the last two decades of the twentieth century. There were substantial advancements in marine science during this period, but they did not inspire the masses with visions of great discovery. The period was largely one of percolation, which is a necessary part of the discovery process. It takes time to brew the perfect cup. Consider the US Navy, for example. During this period it shifted its operational focus from blue to coastal waters. This changed the focus of military oceanography and initiated a renaissance in the development of coastal monitoring and surveillance technologies. But are you aware of them? Perhaps not, and as a result you may not realize that the lottery for the enlightened is once again building its pot of ocean gold for those who position themselves to be in the right field at the right time. The next defining moment in our view of the sea lies just in front of us, not just behind.

Part One:

The Ocean We Know

Chapter One:

Bounded by Time and Space

We categorize hurricanes by the magnitude of their winds, but we remember them by the extent of their water-induced destruction. The two environments, atmosphere and ocean, are linked like conjoined twins.

Decades after his American debut, Jacques Cousteau's subsea view of the sea became common, but it remained incomplete. The restricted value of the scuba diver's view is evident when we consider the profession of meteorology. If meteorologists could only tell you what the atmosphere is doing right now and could only talk about the bit of sky they see with their own eyes, would you listen to them or read their reports? All life depends on the atmosphere, but I do not need someone to tell me I am standing in the rain. I am not interested in the meteorologist's personal view of the sky.

Meteorology is an integral component of our daily routine because it forecasts the future state of the atmosphere. A meteorologist transports our environmental awareness, but not our bodies, into a future time and provides a spatial perspective that greatly exceeds our own. A weather forecast takes us beyond our personal dimensions, as defined by time and space. Few people view their surroundings in such terms, but time and space represent the boundaries of our existence. They are also the essence of meteorology and oceanography, which focus on the dynamics of the atmosphere and ocean.

We seldom think of Earth's environmental phenomena–whether atmospheric, aquatic or terrestrial–as having temporal and spatial scales. Intuitively, we think of environmental processes with respect to our personal boundaries–our personal scales of time and space, such as 'I am standing in the rain', or Jacques Cousteau observing the waters off Assumption Island to be fantastically clear. It is unnatural for scuba divers to look around and think they are in a water mass influenced by uncommon biophysical and biogeochemical processes. Even marine biologists do not think like that, but oceanographers do and so do meteorologists.

Oceanography is walking in the path of meteorology. Like the atmosphere, the ocean varies in both time and space and involves environmental phenomena that we cannot appreciate with the human eye. Like meteorologists, oceanographers desire the means to forecast the future state of the environment. This has immense practical application, particularly with respect to national defense and homeland security. No one doubts the value of forecasting the future state of the atmosphere–our weather–because everyone is surrounded by air, but few appreciate the value of forecasting the future state of the ocean. Thus, meteorology is not a random choice when exemplifying the limitations of the scuba view. The two environments, atmosphere and ocean, are linked like conjoined twins. Neither could survive in their present form without the other. They are separate entities with a critical bond, which oceanographers call the air-sea interface.

Some countries, such as the United States, realize the atmosphere and ocean are linked inextricably; thus they operate combined meteorology and oceanography centers rather than separate atmospheric weather forecasting and operational oceanography centers. Other countries, such as Canada, do this within their military but not within their civilian counterpart. Today, all nations understand that the ocean is but a component of a planetary network of atmospheric, oceanic, and terrestrial processes, each of which inter-relates and varies in time and space. Eventually, countries such as

Canada will need to update their civilian infrastructure as it becomes increasingly impractical to manage.

Meteorology and oceanography are also on different paths of development. Unlike atmospheric forecasting, ocean forecasting is at an embryonic stage, although the concept is not new. Richard Nixon inferred this in 1970 when he announced the formation of the US National Oceanic and Atmospheric Administration (NOAA). In meteorology we first developed the means to forecast the weather. Now, we are advancing our ability to understand atmospheric variability on climatic scales, in support of our understanding of climate change issues. In oceanography, we sort of did it the other way around. We studied its large scale processes first. Now, we are developing the means to forecast its behavior at the finer scales of time and space.[6] In both cases, however, the climate change solution eludes us.

To appreciate why the sea has so much influence upon the atmosphere and vice versa, consider the dimensions of the marine environment. It covers seventy percent of the planet's surface, but an ocean is about one thousand times wider than it is deep. The oceanographer Ian Robinson notes that the aspect ratio of the ocean is about the same as a puddle in the road.[7] This analogy helps us appreciate the extensive influence of the ocean's boundaries–the atmosphere above and the land below and beside.

The sea has massive surface area in direct contact with the atmosphere. As a result, the sea provides eighty-six percent of Earth's evaporation and receives seventy-eight percent of its precipitation. Much of the atmosphere's influence upon our daily lives is a result of air-sea interactions. We all realize that we need water to live, but few

---

[6] W. Munk, "The Evolution of Physical Oceanography in the Last Hundred Years," *Oceanography: The Official Magazine of the Oceanography Association* (March 2002).

[7] Ian S. Robinson, *Measuring the Oceans from Space: The Principles and Methods of Satellite Oceanography* (Chichester: Springer-Praxis, 2004), 78.

of us are aware that from a volume perspective, the exchange of water between ocean and atmosphere is much greater than the exchange of water between land and lakes and land and sea.

Oceanographers expand our understanding of how and why the sea varies in time and space. Operational oceanography is the application of this knowledge to maritime activities. Someday, it will follow its environmental cousin, meteorology, into six o'clock news and weather channels. Eventually, the word *operational* will become redundant, as is the case in meteorology. The public associates the word *weather* with the atmosphere. Nevertheless, the ability to routinely forecast short-term changes in the ocean is within sight, although not everyone agrees as to what we should call this emerging activity. I once received an email from a meteorologist displeased with an editorial I had written for a trade magazine, in which I used the phrase *ocean weather forecasting*. He advised that the word *weather* only pertains to the atmosphere. I replied by asking him to consider the term *computer virus*.

Language changes with innovation and the era of ocean weather forecasting is upon us. The military is on the forefront of this field because having advanced knowledge of the state of the sea provides a military advantage. It is the essence of the emerging field of *ocean intelligence*, the primary purpose of which is to secretly deliver environmental information of strategic or tactical value to deployed forces, such as those aboard submarines or engaged in mine countermeasure or amphibious operations. As much of this knowledge exists within the classified world, you may not be aware of the ocean intelligence sector or even the civilian aspects of ocean weather forecasting. The two sectors feed into each other in a symbiotic relationship so fundamental that it influences the very definition of the word *oceanography*.

Most countries have competent meteorological forecasting capabilities, but no country has yet mastered ocean forecasting. Several western countries, most notably the United States and France, are on the vanguard of this emerging field. They attained this position by capitalizing on four areas of innovation that either advanced or matured in the 1990s: Earth-observing satellites, supercomputers, mathematical models of environmental processes, and the Internet. In oceanography, the word *mesoscale* means on the order of tens to a few hundred kilometers in size, and days to 100 days in duration. For example, oceanographers sometimes characterize mesoscale oceanic eddies as being on the order of 100 km and 100 days in space and time. My point is that even in the United States and France our ability to forecast the behavior of the sea at mesoscale, or smaller than mesoscale, has yet to mature. Similarly, techniques used to forecast the atmosphere have yet to mature at *all* practical scales of time and space. To confirm this, just ask yourself whether your local weatherperson has ever issued an incorrect forecast for your area. For the billons of citizens who live the coastal life, this is a frequent occurrence because on the coast, a meteorologist must also account for influences of the adjacent sea, and that is something we are still working on.

Regardless of whether you live in a coastal community, your attention is captured by the land falling of large hurricanes and typhoons. We categorize hurricanes by the magnitude of their winds, but we remember them by the extent of their water-induced destruction. Many hurricane-related deaths are attributed to drowning. For example, in 2005 Hurricane Katrina devastated New Orleans and surrounding areas and is on record as one of the worst natural disasters in U.S. history. Although it attained Category 5 wind strength prior to landfall, it landed as a Category 3 hurricane. Most of the loss of life and property was a result of accompanying storm surge, not the wind itself. The sea rose to such great height that it breached levees and overran the beach zone. Waterfront property became sea itself in a matter of minutes to hours.

Hurricanes originate in the Atlantic Ocean and East Pacific– north of the equator. If a similar type of event originates in the remainder of the Pacific Ocean, or anywhere within the Indian Ocean, then it is called a typhoon. They do not occur in the cold waters of the Arctic and Southern oceans because the surfaces of these oceans lack the heat required to fuel a hurricane or typhoon. This is one of the reasons why the US National Oceanic and Atmospheric Administration (NOAA) operates a constellation of polar-orbiting, sea-surface temperature satellite sensors that monitor the five oceans of Earth twenty-four hours per day, seven days per week. As hurricanes and typhoons draw their energy from the sea, you need to know the temperature of the ocean along the system's track in order to accurately forecast its strength.

A hurricane is a rare event in Nova Scotia, where I live, as most pass by offshore or fall on the eastern seaboard of the United States. Only eleven have landed in the past fifty years and only thirty-four hurricane-force wind events have fallen in the last one and a half centuries.[8] But one is enough. In 2003, Hurricane Juan came ashore about twenty kilometers from my home. It hit as a Category 2 hurricane, just one level less than Katrina, but the extent of Juan's damage and devastation was a fraction of Katrina's. The water rose such that I lost my wharf, boat ramp, and almost two feet of foreshore–and I was not alone. The damage caused by Juan had not been experienced in Nova Scotia since Hurricane Edna struck in 1954, but few of the residents who experienced Hurricane Juan realize that abnormally high ocean water temperatures off New England, which lies south of Nova Scotia, caused the unusual strength that triggered this rare level of destruction in eastern Canada.

Generally, hurricanes weaken as they move from warm tropical and subtropical waters to the cool temperate waters that reside just off eastern Canada. Hurricane Juan formed 600 kilometers southeast of Bermuda as a result of a meteorological anomaly that

---

[8] Hurricane statistics courtesy of Chris Fogarty, Canadian Hurricane Center, Dartmouth.

formed off the coast of Africa several days earlier. It proved to be about thirty percent more destructive than predicted by Environment Canada's weather model, based on historical water temperatures. Such climatological data are averages over periods of years to decades or longer. They provide a first guess on synoptic (i.e. very large) scales but can be inaccurate for a specific point in time and space. Real-time data generated by environmental sensors, on the other hand, reflect actual conditions at a given time and location. Among these, satellite-based sensors have the greatest impact upon how the public sees large-scale environmental events. Unfortunately, people do not realize these Earth-observing satellite sensors must be calibrated and validated with data collected by sensors located on earth. Unless of course they are meteorologists or oceanographers, or have watched the movie *The Day After Tomorrow*. Then, they realize why nations spend millions of dollars to maintain such earth-based sensors and they understand we need more of them.

The Hollywood drama *The Day After Tomorrow* portrays relationships between time and space for synoptic scale atmospheric and oceanic events, albeit mostly fictional. A climate change model developed by Jack Hall, played by actor Dennis Quaid, is adapted to replicate and forecast catastrophic changes in the weather of the atmosphere and ocean. By developing a model that explains what sensors mounted on offshore buoys are observing, he is able to identify the cause of the catastrophic changes. If you use Google Earth to view waters off the east coast of the United States, you will notice offshore symbols that designate the location of these buoys, at least some of them. When you click on a symbol, you will see real-time environmental data for that location. You will notice, however, that there are very few of these buoys, and therefore environmental forecasting agencies must also rely on climatological data and models.

As portrayed in *The Day After Tomorrow*, the sea involves environmental processes that vary on synoptic and indeed hemispheric scales. In this case, Jack Hall speculates that the North Atlantic Current has shut down as a result of a massive input of freshwater produced by polar ice melting. This part is probably not fiction, as it is believed to have already occurred, albeit ten to twelve thousand years ago. An abnormally massive layer of freshwater floating on the surface of the North Atlantic Ocean has the potential to shut off mixing of deep waters with surface waters, thereby shutting down transfer of heat to the atmosphere in high latitudes.[9] The heat remains trapped in the deep ocean and sea-surface temperatures decrease, which in turn affects atmospheric processes.

In addition to causing him to warn the president of the United States of pending doom, Jack's forecast leads him on a mission to rescue his son Sam (Jake Gyllenhaal), who has a hypothermia-induced snuggle with the rather attractive Laura (Emmy Rossum) while waiting for dad to save them from seemingly certain death. Purists within the science community roll their eyes at such artistic portrayals of science and environmental models, but there is no denying that by reaching his son in the nick of time Jack Hall touches the heart of every parent while teaching us that the atmosphere and ocean are linked on hemispheric scales through cause and effect. In so doing, he raises awareness of the humongous spatial scales at which global warming can influence planet Earth, and he clearly shows the ocean as playing a critical role in the lives of all who inhabit Earth. Understanding these environmental relationships was a major post-Jacques-Cousteau-era advancement in meteorology and oceanography.

This two-hour movie provides more insight into ocean forecasting and the synoptic-scale dynamics of our environment than I received in three years of high school science classes. In defense of

---

[9] R.W. Schmitt and E. Montgomery, "Salinity: A Missing Piece in the Climate Puzzle," *Backscatter: The Official Magazine of the Alliance for Marine Remote Sensing Association* (Summer 2000), 10-16.

my high school curriculum, however, it focused on reality whereas the movie included such far-fetched scenarios as cold-core hurricanes.

Inferred in Jack's work is the role played by sea salt. Density-driven transport of seawater is a function of temperature, salinity (i.e. salt concentration) and depth. In this case, the term freshwater refers to seawater that has extremely low salt concentration. When seawater freezes, it expels its salt. When sea ice melts, it results in fresh, cool surface water until such time that it mixes with warmer saltwater. This subject seems esoteric until you consider the facts that sound waves are used to operate and detect submarines, and acoustic sensors are strongly influenced by variations in water density. Of the three–temperature, water pressure (i.e. depth), and salinity–temperature dominates sound speed variations in about the upper kilometer of the water column. Pressure is the dominant variable below this depth. Thus, measuring variations in water temperature is a fundamental component of antisubmarine warfare operations. Using sea-surface temperature sensors mounted on satellites to help forecast hurricanes is just one application of such sensors.

Worldwide, there are more than three thousand autonomous floats operating within the five oceans of Earth that automatically measure temperature and salinity while oscillating up and down within the sea. Once back on the surface, they relay their data to national environmental centers via data communications satellites. If you would like to see where these floats are right now, just click on http://w4.jcommops.org/website/Argo/ viewer.htm, or to see how the floats work and to view their location in Google Earth access http://www.argo.net/.

In the movie, when the normal transfer of heat and salt shuts down, the sea rises twenty-five feet off Nova Scotia. Rising water floods New York City and the cessation of heat transfer causes the northern hemisphere to go into an almost instantaneous ice age. Canada is transformed into a nation-wide hockey rink, which initially a percentage of Canadians may find appealing. This movie is fictional and although its producers found more offshore buoys than I am aware of, I like it because it demonstrates, as advised by Rachel Carson in the early 1960s, that our environment determines our destiny, not vice versa. We pollute lakes, streams, oceans and the atmosphere but it is only within the last few decades that we have realized we may be influencing hemispheric-scale processes, perhaps irrevocably. Environmental modeling techniques, and Earth-observing satellite sensors that observe mesoscale and larger-scale processes, are the porthole to this new view, and perhaps our survival.

There lies the dilemma. We grew up with Jacques Cousteau's limited scuba view of the sea, but in order to move beyond Cousteau we need a captivating alternative. As in the past, the film and television industries appear to be taking the lead on this. Obviously, they consulted with environmental scientists when developing the script for *The Day After Tomorrow*. Note, for example, in addition to showing the spectacular view from space and the role of environmental forecasting models, the movie identifies the critical role and limited availability of powerful mainframe computers. This is one of the reasons why our ability to model the sea for operational forecasting purposes is several years behind our ability to model the atmosphere.

Obviously, there is much left to do with respect to understanding large-scale environmental processes. However, as a sailor and coastal dweller, it is the air-sea-land interactions that occur on temporal scales of minutes to hours and spatial scales of tens of meters to kilometers, that cause me and my fellow sailors to keep an eye on the weather. We have to, as there is no accurate public forecast for such events. In other words, there is a need for sensors, platforms, and environmental models that detect and monitor relatively fine-scale environmental events, as well as the means to deliver the resulting information to citizens in real time–as the event is unfolding, and preferably before such time. Imagine receiving a Tweet during a cloudy but dry noontime, advising that your end of the city will experience a downpour in thirty minutes, but the remainder of your Saturday will be warm and dry. Would this information influence your daily routine? Would you take your laundry off the line, and when the downpour struck, if you did not receive this fine-scale forecast would you cancel the barbecue with friends you had planned for that evening?

This environmental shortcoming landed in my living room one Saturday in September, except I experienced the marine version. I was sitting at home with my then toddler son, looking out our living room window and idly watching our sailboat at its mooring in the cove, while wishing the gulls would stop pooping on our wharf. The seemingly protected waters of the cove were calm with winds on the adjacent St. Margaret's Bay at about ten knots. The sky was moderate and to my eye provided no warning of what was about to hit us.

The wind rose. Although a sailor for thirty years, even in the comfort and apparent safety of my living room I was startled by how quickly it changed. The accompanying rain blasted my expansive living room window while tell-tale signs of wind streaks started to form on the waters of the cove, all on the order of minutes. The window heaved in gusts of wind. 'It will break', I thought, but as I considered moving my son away from the window, my attention was drawn to the cove itself.

The wind grabbed the furled foresail of my sailboat. Its top partially unfurled and then filled. The boat was now sailing, unmanned and tugging at its mooring in a back-and-forth motion, like an excited dog on a staked leash. I was stunned with disbelief and I knew my pride and my son's joy was in trouble.

I could not get to the boat. The trip required less than two hundred feet of rowing from shore, to save a sail and furling worth several thousand dollars. If the boat broke free of its mooring, then costs would soar and a new hazard to navigation would be upon us. But experience told me to stay put as a ten foot open row boat is no match for such wind, and neither is my swimming ability.

The event passed as quickly as it came. Window intact. Toddler son excited but safe. Foresail flapping gently in a light breeze, with the boat itself standing at its mooring like a horse awaiting its mount. Thankfully, we were not at sea when it hit. The impact could have been disastrous as I did not see it coming. The time-space scales of such environmental events are too small to be captured accurately by environmental models designed to deliver regional-scale weather forecasts. As a result, unless you live by or sail the seas, knowledge of such events rarely reaches your ears or eyes. You can sometimes witness symptoms of such events by logging onto websites of agencies that use Doppler radars. With this land-based microwave sensor you can watch approaching rain and snow squalls in near-real time and at relatively small spatial scales. Certain high-resolution satellite sensors also pick up such events, but not with the temporal resolution of these Doppler radars.

The finer the time-space scales of the air-sea interaction, the finer the model resolution required to forecast it, the greater the amount of data and computer power required to run the model and the greater the cost of setting it up and running it. We are installing the ocean-observing systems required to drive, constrain and validate these models, but it is only within the last few years that we acquired widely available and relatively inexpensive data communications infrastructure that forecasting agencies require to put information in our hands in the required time frame, format and price. It is all part of the percolator of environmental invention, working its way towards the next great innovation and resulting new view of the sea.

Chapter Two:

Ocean Observing

During the twentieth century, we realized that in order to obtain a comprehensive understanding of the sea, we must observe it with something other than the human eye, and must use a vantage point other than the surface of the sea.

In order to model a dynamic environment, we must first identify the forces that drive it. When we develop better marine models, it means we have a better understanding of the sea, although it could also be a result of better modeling techniques. Once we know what causes the sea to behave the way it does, in time and space, we have the means to assess the impact of internal and external forces, such as global warming of the atmosphere, melting of the polar ice caps, human effluents and excessive commercial fishing. But without direct observations of the environment, which are used to constrain, calibrate and validate the model, a mathematical model is simply an academic exercise.

It is a cyclical procedure in which better data result in better models, which in turn result in better understanding. Eventually, it gets to the point where the models tell oceanographers where and when to place their environmental sensors for better results. This is called *adaptive sampling*. During the twentieth century, we realized that in order to obtain a comprehensive understanding of the sea, we must observe it with something other than the human eye, and must use a vantage point other than the surface of the sea.

Rachel Carson, Jacques Cousteau, James Bond author Ian Fleming, and my navy father all formed their view of the sea around the middle of the twentieth century. With each account of the sea, whether it be from a science writer, explorer, novelist, or sailor, we witness a particular view. But what I, you, my father, the US Navy, or anyone else sees with the human eye is but a piece of an environmental puzzle. Think of the reality police television show that searches for the suspect at night from a helicopter. The woods appear empty until the pilot uses a thermal infrared sensor to view the same area. Suddenly, we discover the woods are not as they appear to the human eye.

If this scene was played out at sea and the suspect was a ship full of refugees consumed by a potentially pandemic flu, an Al-Qaida controlled submarine, a pending category five hurricane, a tsunami, an immobilizing ice floe, a grounded super-tanker, or a bloom of lethal algae, homeland security and environmental agencies that guard our sovereign waters would likely turn on a buffet of sensors. There are so many sensors, and a helicopter is not the only available platform for them. What you place the sensor on is as critical as the sensor itself in terms of orchestrating your view of the sea.

For any one of these hypothetical maritime scenarios, we would use a combination of sensors and platforms. During my father's Royal Navy days, you could sail the seas and have a good chance of not being detected outside of a shipping channel. It would be naive to think this today. If a substantive vessel is sailing the waters of an advanced nation and not reporting in, then that nation is either watching it directly or covertly detecting its environmental signature.

Avoiding detection by such systems is central to modern naval warfare and maritime security, and it is not just about detecting ships. It is also about detecting and monitoring the state of the sea and the atmosphere above it. The marine environment affects the performance of ships, but it also affects the performance of sensors and weapons. As a result, having advanced knowledge of the dynamics of the sea, through application of ocean-observing technologies, provides military advantage. Most of these technologies did not exist during Jacques Cousteau's days in the French Navy or during my father's days in the Royal Navy.

The key enabler that started to occur around the middle of the twentieth century is adequate sampling.[10] This is why we studied large-scale oceanic processes first. The technologies and models required to permit ocean weather forecasting did not come into their own until the latter quarter of the twentieth century. Historically, the ocean was sampled from ships. During and after World War II, we developed the means to sample it effectively from offshore buoys, but it is impractical to deploy enough ships and buoys to adequately sample and forecast the state of the ocean at mesoscale and finer scales.

Like meteorologists observing the atmosphere, oceanographers employ a variety of sensors and platforms. Co-location of these sensors and platforms in a specific region of the marine environment is called an *ocean-observing system*. Such systems involve sensors mounted on five types of platforms–satellites, aircraft, surface and subsea platforms, and shore based installations. Numerous types of sensors can be mounted on each type of platform. Sensors located in the sea (i.e. in situ) are the most prevalent and are the only ones that routinely sample well below the surface. Among these, Fredrick Hunt's beloved acoustic sensors are probably the most common. Unfortunately, sensors located within the water only tell you what the ocean is doing at the sensor's specific location, similar to the scuba diver's personal view of the sea. Alternatively, satellites, aircraft, and certain shore-based installations provide wide-area views of the sea, which means they are capable of capturing environmental processes that occur at large spatial scales, like hurricanes.

---

[10] Munk. "The Evolution of Physical Oceanography in the Last Hundred Years."

As the twentieth century was coming to an end, advanced nations started to deploy coastal ocean-observing systems, The most advanced of these, such as the University of Victoria's Neptune Canada and VENUS programs, involve all five observing platforms and hundreds of sensors. "Since 2006, VENUS has proven the concepts and technologies for cabled observatories," advises Scott McLean, director of the Centre for Enterprise and Engagement at Ocean Networks Canada. He also notes that "Neptune Canada is the first regional-scale underwater ocean observatory network to plug directly into the Internet".

NASA's 1978 launch of the first ocean-observing satellite was a breakthrough in environmental science and a defining moment in the development of oceanography. On 27 June 1978, NASA forever changed the way we view the sea when the Jet Propulsion Laboratory in California launched four sea-viewing microwave sensors on Seasat. A few months later, NOAA launched the first of its fourth-generation thermal infrared sea-surface temperature sensors. Then, in an inspiring demonstration of the depth of the United States' space program at the time, on 24 October, just four months after Seasat's launch, NASA's Goddard Space Flight Center launched the Nimbus-7 satellite.

These spaceborne environmental sampling technologies have since become so common that you can click on the website of any national weather forecasting agency and find satellite images of mesoscale and synoptic-scale atmospheric and marine features. Among these, the Gulf Stream is the most obvious marine feature off the east coast of North America. Henry Stommel, the physical oceanographer from Woods Hole, Massachusetts, is credited with unlocking the mysteries of this so-called "western boundary current" during the mid-twentieth century. This massive current bounds the North Atlantic Ocean and the coast of North America. Satellite images show that its waters are warm because it starts in the sub-tropical waters of the Caribbean and Gulf of Mexico before flowing northward off the east coast of the United States. Its northern branch eventually turns east and fans across the Atlantic Ocean towards the coast of Europe. The warm waters of the Gulf Stream and the air-sea interactions that occur above them contribute to the relatively warm climate of sections of the coast of Europe. The equivalent latitudes of Canada's east coast are influenced more by the frigid waters of the Labrador Current and therefore are significantly colder than their European counterparts, although other environmental factors are involved as well.

The Gulf Stream can also contribute to poor weather conditions that occur along the Atlantic coast of the United States, but the extent of its influence upon our lives goes well beyond the weather. The Gulf Stream occurs over such a large area and with such intensity that inter-annual changes in its position cause sea levels off northern New England to vary by up to ten centimeters (i.e. about four inches). The Gulf Stream also meanders and in so doing pieces of it shear off and travel towards the coast of North America as rings of water known as warm-core rings, so named for the ring's water temperature relative to its engulfing colder coastal waters. In addition to relatively warm temperatures, these mesoscale features cause current shear and influence life in their immediate area, as can cold-core rings of coastal water that become entrapped within the Gulf Stream. The US Navy and Canadian Armed Forces routinely monitor both types of rings as they influence the performance of acoustic sensors and therefore affect submarine and antisubmarine warfare operations. Civilian agencies also monitor these phenomena as they affect both a vessel's travel time and the weather it will encounter along its journey.

The features of the Gulf Stream vary at scales so large that we cannot see them in their entirety with our eyes, from shore or sea, and neither can any other Earth-bound sensor. In addition to spatial scales, larger ocean phenomena tend to change over longer time scales, although it can be misleading to make such generalities. The polar ice caps, for example, change over periods of decades to millennia, but aspects of the Gulf Stream may change over just a few days.

A key aspect of effective environmental observing systems is the perishable nature of critical data. A sailor can store a nautical chart for years, but environmental information can lose its operational value within hours. The fresher the environmental information, the greater its operational value, and if it pertains to national security, then the more guarded it becomes. On naval websites you will find satellite images and products produced by environmental models, but not the navy's finest-scale output, and by scale I refer to both time and space. Such are the juicy bits that feed the ocean intelligence community. You can also view satellite imagery of the coastal zone via the free version of Google Earth, but for security reasons, financial implications, data volume, copyright, or some other practical reason, you will not find satellite images from all types of ocean-observing satellite sensors.

Proliferation of these and other such sensors has roots in how the sea affects our lives. Offshore tsunami warning sensors, for example, were few in number or absent in many critical areas until December 2004, when an earthquake-driven tsunami produced waves reportedly up to one hundred feet in height and caused the death of approximately two hundred thousand people living in coastal areas of the Indian Ocean, in addition to billions of dollars of damage and billions more in humanitarian aid. Citizens of India, Indonesia, Sri Lanka and Thailand suffered the worst.

In addition to humanitarian aid, the developed world responded with ocean-observing systems that detect and monitor tsunamis and coastal storm surge. They comprise sensors, platforms, environmental models and the means to distribute information in operational time frames. We have been aware of tsunamis since we first lived on the shores of the sea, and tsunami-detecting sensors have been available for decades, but it required a catastrophic event that captured global media attention to implement the appropriate network of ocean-observing sensors and platforms.

The earthquake and resulting tsunami that occurred in Japan in March 2011 had horrific consequences, but did you notice how quickly neighboring nations observed the tsunami's extended path? Did you see resulting satellite images and trajectory forecasts on TV and the Internet, within minutes and hours of the tsunami's creation?

Similarly, in the late twentieth century, hurricane activity and human populations increased along the Atlantic coast of America, yet human mortality as a result of hurricanes decreased during the last century. Sensors, environmental models, and forecasting agencies are largely responsible for this desirable inverse relationship. In both cases, Japan and America, response was quick because the models and required sensors and platforms were already in place and programmed for operational response. These systems were unable to save thousands of lives in northeastern Japan because a tsunami travels so quickly. Residents were so close to the source that the system only provided emergency response agencies with minutes of warning for this area. To appreciate Japan's extensive environmental monitoring and forecasting capabilities, however, log onto http://www.jma.go.jp/ en/quake/. As was the case for rapid advancement of oceanography during World War II and the Cold War, security of life and country is the driving force behind this development. Governments talk about protecting the environment, but when it comes to maritime security, they act.

Maritime search and rescue operations also require ocean-observing systems. Synoptic maps of surface water temperature help to estimate the effect of hypothermia on survival time, but the primary environmental need pertains to surface currents. When a person falls overboard or a ship goes down, that person or the life raft keeping them afloat does not remain stationary. Floating objects move with the surface of the sea, driven by wind, tides, and surface currents. Having the ability to determine the direction and speed of the drifting target can make the difference between saving a life and recovering a body. Without models of trajectory, which incorporate data collected by ocean-observing systems, such operations may inadvertently deploy aircraft and ships in the wrong direction.

NOAA and the US Coast Guard recently implemented an inspirational search and rescue application for one of these ocean-observing technologies: shore-based high frequency radar, which measures surface currents.[11] In the US, most of these systems are called CODAR SeaSondes®, or just SeaSonde. Of course, the SeaSonde will not in itself attract broad public interest until it results in saving lives. This has yet to happen, but when it does, the media will show images of search and rescue personnel dropping from helicopters in hellish seas, while interviewing survivors and hugging offspring. A few years thereafter, we will deem this emerging technology *indispensable*.

Collectively, regional maritime search and rescue assets cost tens to hundreds of thousands of dollars to operate per day and orders of magnitude more in capital costs. They also require skilled hands and steady nerves in the adverse weather conditions that often prevail during a search and rescue operation. I cringe whenever an adventurer sets off from the coast of Newfoundland in an attempt to cross the Atlantic Ocean on a paddleboard or some other vessel of seemingly inadequate design. It is not only the person's life that will be in danger if the adventure runs afoul. Yet, despite massive capital expenditures and the unselfish bravery of coast guard personnel, maritime search and rescue operations are strikingly inadequate in many parts of the coastal zone. I learned this one spring while searching the shores of Barbados.

---

[11]. http://www.noaanews.noaa.gov/stories2009/20090504_ioss.html. For another perspective on this subject see B. Venkataraman, "Finding Order in the Apparent Chaos of Currents," *New York Times,* September 28, 2009.

Over a four-day period in early June, my taxi driver and I drove along the southeastern coast of Barbados and among the streets of its capital city of Bridgetown. 'Junior', as his friends call him, is calm for a man who spends his life in traffic. When we first met, I was sitting in the back seat, viewing him in profile. I could not see his facial expressions as we talked about the beaches of Barbados and the bit of the Caribbean Sea that we saw through the taxi's windows. As we drove towards Barbados' Coastal Zone Management Unit, the tone of the conversation changed from common tourist-type banter to knowledge and perceptions of the sea. Familiar ground for an oceanographer, but without warning Junior broadsided me with his account of a voyage to the edge of life—his own life.

Even as he told his story of being lost at sea for thirteen days, there was little emotion in his voice until he mentioned his family. He gave up a career as a "big fish" seaman to be with his family. They were the reason why he looked forward to Father's Day this upcoming weekend, and they were on his mind one year previous, almost to the day, when he thought his Father's Day at sea would be the last he spent alive.

Marlin, tuna, dolphin, shark, it made no difference to Junior as he joined Captain Sean and two fellow crewman for hook and line fishing in waters off his home country. They dropped baited lines suspended from buoys and returned later to pick them up, hopefully with something big attached. Junior was in his sixth season of fishing when the lone Volvo engine of the fishing boat *Labor of Love* gave out. The forty-six foot blue and grey boat carried four berths plus the Captain's bunk on the upper deck, but not the parts required to replace a cracked piston head.

When the engine started to overheat, the captain radioed in to the Barbados Coast Guard. The boat was only 111 nautical miles from Barbados, but in rough seas and headwinds they were advised it could take one to two days to reach them from the coast guard's

HMBS *Pelican* base in Spring Garden, just a short distance from Bridgetown's renowned cricket oval.

The radio lost power two days after the engine did, without a coast guard vessel in sight. Drifting with wind and currents at a rate of about thirty nautical miles per day, they lost contact with the coast guard while maintaining radio contact with fellow fishing boats, until the radio lost power. "A boat full of fish on its way home will stop and tow you in, but they can't go home empty handed. They can't afford to spend their fuel to go and look for you with an empty boat," Junior explained. He had been towed in several times during his years at sea, as had many others. It was not an uncommon occurrence among the fleet, thus not a cause for panic.

As his story unfolded, I began to appreciate why Junior was such a calm man. Stress is relative and the lost engine was not their primary concern at this point. With 3,000 gallons remaining in the boat's 5,000 gallon freshwater tank, they had plenty of water, but their boat was no longer where they had told the coast guard they were located. Their position had changed with the wind and sea, and it was the seas that concerned them now and the shipping lanes they drifted among. Without power, at night they were invisible to large ships sailing among them. Even during the day they were incapable of getting out of harm's way. In addition to the danger of being cut up by a freighter or tanker, they could run aground on an offshore reef. Without power for steerage, the *Labor of Love* also took the sea broadside as she drifted freely. "It was the short seas that had us worried, waves about ten to twelve feet that can capsize a boat if taken the wrong way." It was rough, day after day. "Everything had to be tied down."

The captain decided to keep three lookouts around the clock. "We took turns sleeping for three hours at a time" Junior advised. To help pass the time they fished, and the fishing was good. "There were plenty of curious fish about us," because the boat was drifting free with no noisy engine to scare them away.

On their tenth day adrift, a fishing boat loaded with tuna spotted them and came within hail. They were on their way home to Grenada, which lies about 125 nautical miles to the southwest of Barbados. The *Labor of Love's* distance from its home port had not changed greatly in ten days but its relative position had. A 125 mile circumference around Barbados represents a lot of sea to search.

Getting a line to the stricken boat in short seas was no easy task, and was only accomplished after one of the crew volunteered to swim the line across. This in itself can be dangerous on the high seas, thus rarely attempted without a line attached to the swimmer. Once attached by the line, the Granada boat towed the Barbadians for two days before they had to set them adrift again. If they had continued, they would have run out of fuel before reaching port. A day later the Grenadians returned with a trawler and towed the *Labor of Love* and its crew to a second life. Before setting them adrift, the rescuers had provided the Barbadian crew with a GPS-enabled tracking device, to facilitate their rediscovery. Out of gratitude, the captain and crew of the *Labor of Love* gave their entire catch to Grenada's hospital and anyone else who wanted it.

When Junior first spoke of his days of survival I was speechless, but thereafter I wanted to know every detail. It wasn't just because I wanted to tell his story. I am also a sailor and when you sail the high seas, at some point disaster at sea will enter your mind. Professional sailors, like my father, weave safety into their daily routine. The only bit of seamanship advice my navy father ever gave me pertained to safety at sea. He once told me that when I was looking for something to do during idle hours at sea on a large ship, I should practice getting from one deck to the next with my eyes closed. It simulates the light level in a companionway full of smoke.

When I finished my meeting that first day at Barbados' Coastal Zone Management Unit, Junior drove me to the very coast guard base he had pinned his hopes of rescue upon almost one year previous. Coincidentally, I had a pre-arranged appointment with the base commander to discuss marine monitoring and modeling in support of search and rescue operations. "This was my dream", Junior said as he drove through the base security gate. "I wanted to be in the coast guard, but I'm too old to get in now."

Despite their failure to rescue him, Junior harbored no ill will toward the coast guard. He knew they were an organization of limited means, and the Grenada Coast Guard had housed and fed him while he waited to return to Bridgetown. Even when they knew where the *Labor of Love* was located, the Grenada Coast Guard could not provide a vessel of sufficient tonnage to tow them in. The Barbados Coast Guard has such boats, but not vessel-locating trajectory analyses software and accompanying surface current data produced by shore-based CODAR SeaSondes. In Junior's case, these techniques would have estimated the *Labor of Love's* trajectory from its last known position as it drifted towards Grenada. Instead, it was sheer luck and the kindness and skills of fellow sailors that allowed Junior to live another Father's Day. Countless others are not so lucky.

In addition to the search and rescue sector, the offshore oil and gas sector relies on ocean-observing systems in the Gulf of Mexico to advise when a rig will be impacted by strong currents and to help mitigate the effects of oil spills. This industry also utilizes ocean-observing networks within the Labrador Sea and Grand Banks to warn of drifting icebergs approaching offshore rigs. Similarly, tuna and albacore industries benefit from maps of surface water temperatures because the locations of these species are related to water temperature. The marine transportation industry uses ocean observing information pertaining to the Gulf Stream to help navigate transatlantic voyages. Being in the correct position relative to the northeastern components of the Gulf Stream, which are known for their strong currents and inclement weather, can save hours to days of unnecessary travel time and thousands of dollars in fuel. Also, vessels of all sizes and purpose benefit from forecasts of wave conditions.

Despite all this capability, we still do not have sufficient sensors and platforms to adequately capture the time-space spectrum of such environmental processes. Given that these processes span orders of magnitude from seconds to decades and from meters to thousands of kilometers, we never will. This is another reason why we have environmental models. They fill in the gaps.

There are also outstanding technical issues. Spaceborne optical sensors, for example, are heavily influenced by atmospheric effects. About ninety-five percent of the signals received by an optical spaceborne sensor come from the atmosphere, not the sea. Thus, accurate accounting of atmospheric effects is a critical requirement for this type of sensor. In addition, most civilian Earth-observing satellite programs have too few satellites in orbit to fully comprehend what is happening in the ocean. This limitation can be diminished by launching a constellation of satellite sensors, but the associated cost is astronomical. Thus, there is a trend toward nations sharing their Earth-observing satellites and the in-water sensors required to calibrate them. Effectively this results in a constellation of sensors and a world-wide movement to cooperatively create a *global-ocean-observing system*.

Basically, what this all means is that each of the sensor/platform combinations complements each other, and marine monitoring is platform limited. In other words, we do not have enough satellites, aircraft, buoys, ships, and towers to adequately observe the marine environment. This led Thomas Curtain of the US Office of Naval Research to state: "With current trends, overall forecasting system advances will be increasingly platform limited."[12] We need environmental models to forecast the state of the marine

---

[12] T.B. Curtin, "Autonomous Oceanographic Sampling Networks: Status Report Through FY 97/QI," in *Rapid Environmental Assessment: Proceedings of Conference on Rapid Environmental Assessment,* eds. E. Pouliquen, A.D. Kirwan Jr., and R.T. Pearson (La Specia, Italy: NATO SACLANT Undersea Research Center, 1997), 153.

environment, and to fill in the gaps between platforms, but they do not replace our need for observations.

Chapter Three:

Matrix of the Sea

....the next time you think about making a noose for an oilman, also make one for yourself, and I am just as guilty as the next. I speculate so are most environmentalists.

As an undergraduate student in Vancouver, British Columbia, I travelled home to Victoria during holidays, reading breaks, and summer vacations. The bus was my preferred mode of transportation because it guaranteed you would get a seat on the ever popular Vancouver to Victoria ferry. It also provided a view to one of the most spectacular stretches of sea you will ever witness, for the meager price of a bus ride. During one of these trips, for example, the pod of killer whales that surfaced about the ferry was so large that the captain slowed his engines.

When returning to Vancouver and once on the mainland again, the bus travels via Tsawwassen and the suburbs of Vancouver. During one such trip, through a window of the bus I saw a man standing in the yard of his home. I remember him because he was servicing his lawn in the rain, while wearing a bright yellow Arnold Palmer golf sweater. Whether he applied fertilizer, herbicide, or insecticide I do not know, but this image remains with me through the decades since. Not because it taught me that golfers in Vancouver view rain as liquid sunshine. Not because Rachel Carson and my university professors taught me that when it rains, these chemicals wash into the groundwater we drink and the sea that affects the air we breathe. I remember it because, like the gardening golfer himself, and others riding by that day, I witnessed an environmental tragedy in the making and thought nothing of it. Regardless of your profession or pastime, we have become accustomed to impacting the ecosystems that sustain our lives.

This scenario is the essence of Rachel Carson's 1962 book, *Silent Spring*, except she focuses more on municipal and industrial applications of pesticides. Although half a century old, the problem continues and the sea is feeling its effect. Within hours, a downpour can change the appearance of nearshore waters from clear to seemingly toxic tea. This discoloration is obvious to the eye and in remote areas may be due to naturally occurring substances found in forests, lakes, and streams. They go by various chemical names and to make matters more confusing, some suspend in water as extremely large complex molecules called colloids. Like an alien travelling to another dimension, they may co-exist in two worlds, partially in the dissolved phase and partially in the solid phase. Upon contact with seawater, they may precipitate entirely into the solid phase and thereby collect on the bottom of nearshore waters.

Hidden within or otherwise associated with these particles and substances are the chemicals we leak onto roads, pour down sinks, use to make clothes clean, dishes sparkle, and toilet-bowls shine. Even those who do not spray lawns, gardens, forests, and fields contribute to the process. All of humanity participates, and my knowledge of this has become a bit of a curse. How many people feel stressed with a sense of environmental danger when they watch a television commercial encouraging you to turn your toilet water blue? When you flush your toilet, what happens to these chemicals?

A downpour of rain is akin to flushing the toilet bowl of the coastal environment, but the relationship between cause and effect is not obvious. While working as a post-doctoral fellow on a coastal oceanography project in Kingston, Jamaica, I had the task of figuring out why sand was disappearing from a beach slated for tourism development. Local scientists determined that the problem was a symptom of a dying coral reef, located just offshore from the beach, but they did not know why the reef was dying.

I worked on the project for over a year, using several hundred thousand dollars in development aid to purchase field equipment and to outfit an oceanographic laboratory. But I could not determine what was happening until I looked through dozens of images acquired by the US Landsat series of Earth-observing satellites. There it was, like a photograph in a family album. On occasion, a bordering river would turn brown. When this water flowed into the adjoining harbor and its approaches, it impacted the fan corals lying just offshore, which previously had dampened the effect of sand-removing wave action. The entire area comprised but a few square kilometers. A quick cross-reference with meteorological data correlated the periods of darkened river water with short periods of heavy rain, occurring on a temporal scale of minutes to hours. Time and space, air and earth, oceanography is always a matter of temporal and spatial variations and the environments that bound the sea.

Having survived gales at sea, I pride myself for not being a fair-weather sailor, but on the shores of a Caribbean island, I had become just that. I did not sample during downpours or shortly thereafter, and thus never captured the biochemical and biophysical effects of this meteorological event. If not for the satellite sensor, I may never have discovered the source of the problem.

We subsequently learned that the discoloration in the river water resulted from industrial activity, whereby heavy rains caused mine tailings to overflow into the river. In a nation desperate for industrial development, one industry was an obstacle to employment in another. With cause and effect not obvious, residents went about their daily lives, like a gardening golfer, seemingly oblivious of the fact that their activities were destroying the sea around them. There is a lesson here for all, not just developing countries. Residents of the Canadian city of Halifax, for example, may not appreciate what happens to their sewage during periods of heavy rain. It does not matter where you reside, east or west, developed or developing, rain flushes all watershed areas. Some cities and companies do an exceptional job of managing their wastes, others not so well. The good, the bad, and the downright ugly do not necessarily divide along lines of development or even law. It is more a matter of education and attitude. We perceive certain activities to be OK because we have engaged in them for generations.

More than eighty percent of coastal pollution is caused by people living in watershed areas that drain into the sea, which includes cities, towns, neighborhoods, and industries located many miles from the sea.[13] The next time the six o'clock news shows a picture of a tanker or oil rig in trouble, remember that the seagoing community itself contributes less than 20 percent of the hydrocarbons entering the sea. A major tanker spill in coastal waters is an environmental tragedy, but so is hundreds of millions of people flushing chemicals down their toilets, sinks and storm drains. Tankers spill a relatively small amount of hydrocarbons when compared to the amount flushed from land-based sources, or spewed into the atmosphere, every second of every hour of every day of every year of every decade since the onset of the industrial revolution. I do not wish to make light of highly-impacting spills, such as the 2010 spill in the Gulf of Mexico, but the next time you think about making a noose for an oilman, also make one for yourself, and I am just as guilty as the next. I speculate so are most environmentalists.

A related issue is the effect of excess nutrients on the growth of marine plants, which are also referred to as phytoplankton, algae, and macrophytes. Worldwide, millions of farmers spread fertilizers on their lands, and private citizens spread fertilizers on house plants, gardens, and lawns, and use nutrient-laced soaps to clean themselves, their clothes, and their possessions. Invariably, a detrimental

---

[13] United Nations Environment Programme, *Global Programme of Action.*

proportion of these nutrients end up in Earth's hydrosphere, including its groundwater, streams, lakes, and seas.

Through a process called eutrophication, plant growth in coastal waters is stimulated by nutrients of anthropogenic source. In other words, human activities cause the plants to bloom to excess. Any nutrient-related activity within a watershed area has the potential of contributing to eutrophication of lakes and sea. You do not need to be within sight of the water to be part of the problem. Out of sight is not synonymous with out of harm's way. Living in a rural area, I often witness people spreading something on their lawns and gardens while standing within view of the well from which they obtain their drinking water.

Although still open to debate, there may be a relationship between eutrophication and the outbreak of toxic algae. These particular species of plants are often referred to as harmful algae, and when they suddenly occur in high concentrations it is called a harmful algae bloom. They can render shellfish poisonous to humans and can lead to depletion of oxygen required by other marine life. Thus, toxic algae can lead to large-scale fish kills, odorous water and ruined beaches. In turn, these symptoms have economic and urban repercussions such as decreases in coastal recreation, tourism, and property values. Another way of stating this is that when we discharge massive amounts of nutrients into coastal areas, we inadvertently ruin the ecosystem we live in, and require to survive.

In the last decade, coastal tourism and recreation experienced a 100 % increase in their combined contribution to the gross domestic product (GDP) of the United States. During the same period, certain traditional coastal industries, such as ship and boat building, experienced declines in their contributions to GDP. This economic shift from goods to services, combined with the fact that about half of the world's population lives within coastal watershed areas, is increasing attention on quality of life in coastal waters, and therefore on programs that monitor water quality. Regional, national and global ocean-observing systems allow managers to view and track the impact of such activities on temporal and spatial scales that could not be monitored comprehensively in Rachel Carson's days. Although Carson raised the alarm, it is probable that in the 1960s even she was unaware of the magnitude of the environmental processes that such actions affect.

Monitoring the flow and impact of pollutants is but one application of ocean observing and environmental modeling, and not all applications pertain to the biology of the sea. It just seems that way because intuitively we view the environment from the perspective of life on Earth. Similarly, not all applications pertain to short-term events. Certain environmental features change on time scales of decades or longer, but we cannot tell they are changing simply by looking at them. Since my beach house was built in the late 1950s, for example, sea level in the vicinity of the adjacent bay has risen by about 20 centimeters (eight inches). I do not sense that mean sea level is rising simply by looking at the sea. This is not something we residents observe, but if you live here long enough you will witness its effect. Eight inches may not seem like much unless spring high tide routinely comes within inches of the top of the 1950s era wall that separates you from the sea, and your foreshore is relatively flat.

Even in this example, it is possible to view the sea from Jacques Cousteau's and Rachel Carson's biological perspective. Sea level rise is associated with melting of the polar ice caps, which scientists argue is a result of global warming, which in turn is associated with increased concentrations of green-house gases (e.g. carbon dioxide) in the atmosphere. Gases present in the atmosphere penetrate surface waters and vice versa. Like all plants, marine plants consume carbon dioxide and therefore play a role in the global carbon cycle. One of the most profound outstanding goals in biological oceanography is to quantify this role. Given the massive expanse of the air-sea interface, there is no doubt that it is significant. This is why academia has such great interest in satellite sensors that quantify the color of the sea. Primarily, in the open ocean variations in water color pertain to variations in phytoplankton.

Although it is natural to view the sea from our personal perspective, this approach impedes our understanding of the ocean because intuitively we do not consider sensors that view the sea at wavelengths invisible to the human eye. Such sensors function outside of the visible light component of the electromagnetic spectrum. Think of the sun, and the fact that it emits more than visible energy. It also, for example, emits energy at ultraviolet frequencies. We do not see ultraviolet energy, but are conscious of its existence due to the harm it can do to our skin. Ultraviolet energy exists at shorter wavelengths than visible energy, just shorter than that of the color violet. Infrared energy, which can be used to detect the temperature of water, borders visible energy at the longer wavelengths. Collectively, ultraviolet, visible, and infrared energy comprise components of the electromagnetic spectrum, but this energy spectrum continues beyond these bands. It also includes energy at frequencies we call microwave energy, which again we cannot see with our eyes. Most adults know how to use a microwave oven, for making things like popcorn. NASA and the space agencies of other nations use microwave energy for numerous other purposes. From my perspective, they use it to detect surface winds, waves, currents, ice, sea height, eddies, ships, oil spills, and the boundaries between land and sea. Like thermal infrared sensors, microwave sensors only detect features on the very surface of the sea, but under certain conditions microwave sensors can detect subsea features such as internal waves and water depth, because under such conditions these features create environmental signatures on the surface of the sea. These signatures are like environmental fingerprints.

In the 1940s the British used radar to detect aircraft, but in 1978 the Americans shot it into space. The rest of the west followed. Today, with sensor names like Alos, Asar, Grace, Jason, Nscat,

Radarsat, Terra, Topex, Lupe and Swot, allied countries and several other nations have discovered there is much more to the microwave band than making popcorn and detecting airplanes. To the untrained eye, images produced by microwave sensors make little if any sense. Our eyes do not see microwave energy and therefore we are not accustomed to how it interacts with our environment. We may, however, harness its benefits by evolving like Neo, a.k.a. Mr. Anderson, in the movie *The Matrix*. There is much more to our surroundings than what we are led to believe by our eyes. Think of the scene in the movie where the character Neo, played by actor Keanu Reeves, finally gets it. He enters a corridor where the walls transform from wood and plaster to fluorescent green waterfalls of computer code that define the walls' composition and spatial and temporal boundaries. You can witness a facsimile of the real thing at the US Naval Research Laboratory at NASA's John C. Stennis Space Flight Center, in Mississippi. Their ocean modeling and visualization room is not a corridor, but the walls of this modest, windowless room are covered by streams of flowing colors displayed on flat-paneled screens. They present the five oceans of Earth in all their glory, in both time and space. The computers that deliver information to these screens run environmental models fed by terabytes of data collected by ocean-observing sensors.

Unlike the movie version, at Stennis you do not see the code itself. When preparing an environmental briefing for operational forces, oceanographers who work at Stennis do not hand out tables of code or sheets of formulas. They hand out pictures and they use color to transform images of invisible energy into intuitive information. At Stennis and in numerous oceanographic centers worldwide, groups of data are assigned a color and co-displayed on now common digital nautical charts. Resulting images are not as intuitive as a photograph and initially they just look like walls of streaming color, until like Neo you get it. In one such view, with your eyes focused on falsely colored images of thermal infrared energy, you can see the otherwise invisible meanderings of the Gulf Stream. This mighty current's spectacular northern wall stands out like a creature in a science fiction flick. It is colored fire-engine red to reflect its relatively warm temperatures. The adjacent chilly waters of the Labrador Sea are a cold steel blue and in between these two extremes lie the aqua-blues, greens and yellows of intermediate temperature waters that flow on and off the coasts of North America.

Color palettes are also used to color images of microwave energy, to show wind patterns across the North Atlantic, variations in sea height caused by warm and cold-core rings and potentially treacherous wave patterns that form at the boundaries of water masses. In every case, they show features not visible to the human eye, as the computer models represent and forecast the sea in four dimensions.

You do not need to travel to Mississippi to see this with your own eyes. To obtain images of sea characteristics detected by invisible energy, click on one of the U.S. Navy's websites, or one of NASA's, NOAA's or the European Space Agency's ocean-related websites. These agencies have extensive ocean-observing programs, as do the space agencies, navies and civilian environmental agencies of France, Japan, China, India and many other countries. When searching these sites you are likely to come across both satellite images and images produced by environmental models that use satellite data. If the website does not specify which you are viewing, it may be difficult to tell them apart.

As you explore these sites, you will observe that in addition to using microwave sensors to detect physical parameters and features, they also use visible sensors to detect biological parameters and features. Depending upon the location, these ocean color sensors are detecting variations in phytoplankton concentration, but the closer to shore the body of water, the greater the influence of terrestrial constituents, such as those of rivers, streams, and groundwater, whether they occur naturally or are caused by humans. When viewing these images you will also notice that, like your eyes, sensors operating in the visible and infrared bands of the spectrum cannot see through clouds or at night, which severely restricts their utility. Microwave sensors can 'see' through clouds and operate at night, which makes for an all-weather, twenty-four hour per day sensing capability.

During the final decade of the twentieth century, as the glory days of Jacques Cousteau began to fade into memory, the spaceborne view changed the way we view the sea. In his biography of Jacques Cousteau, Axel Madsen states that the French adventurer once made the point that the space-based view requires us to conceive the sea's delicate balance not as a separate entity but as a component of the whole planet. We now clearly understand this, but Cousteau's point demonstrates considerable insight. It suggests that although his eyes and cameras were restricted to observing visible light, his lifetime of marine adventure provided exceptional thought on how to view the sea and the rewards that different perspectives may bring. I make this point because Cousteau was criticized for not pursuing the science of the sea, even though he was not trained as a scientist, did not claim to be a scientist, and sometimes brought scientists along on his ship, the *Calypso*.

While working on one of their ABC television episodes, in 1974, Cousteau and his team also worked on a mapping contract for NASA, during which they measured the transparency and reflective properties of sea and sediments.[14] This work was associated with the US Landsat series of Earth-observing satellites, but it is conceivable that data collected by the Cousteau team aided the utility of NASA's 1978 Coastal Zone Color Scanner sensor–the first spaceborne sensor designed to view the color of the sea. Regardless, Jacques Cousteau was among the first to collect ocean color data to calibrate and

---

[14] R. Munson, *Cousteau: The Captain and his World* (New York: William Morrow, 1989), 166.

validate an Earth-observing satellite sensor. According to Munson he was criticized for doing so, as it meant taking time away from his television duties; damned if he did and damned if he did not.

In 1980, months after NASA and NOAA launched inaugural spaceborne ocean-observing sensors, Cousteau stated that the space-based view is essential to oceanographic research. During the decade that followed, his organization signed contracts with both agencies.[15] Cousteau's advanced insight leads me to speculate that throughout their careers, people like Jacques Cousteau and Rachel Carson wondered about the matrix of the sea, how it varies in time and space, and what forces cause such variations. As marine explorers, they asked what made the ocean tick, but at the time they lacked the sensors, models, and computers required to answer such questions comprehensively, at all of the critical scales of time and space. In certain respects, this knowledge continues to elude us.

The spaceborne view of the marine environment shows one hundred and forty million people earning a living from fisheries and aquaculture, thirty percent of the world's oil and gas being extracted by offshore production platforms, and ninety thousand merchant ships supporting these and other forms of commerce. The most recent view also shows wind and tidal energy being harnessed in coastal waters. Yet, the spaceborne view demonstrates that defining the ocean as a means of nutrition, energy, transportation, and warfare is an over-simplification. This long-standing perception is incomplete. It was common when my father was alive and when baby boomers were growing up, but with our present understanding of oceanic processes we have ample grounds to lay this perception to rest. Previously, we focused on what we can get out of the sea, for personal benefit, but now we focus on what we are putting *into* it. Now, ocean-observing sensors and environmental models cause us to think about the impact this has on planetary ecosystems. Now, we all ponder like Rachel

---

[15] Ibid., 231.

Carson, but on much grander scales of time and space than even Carson likely considered. Knowledge gained through our present view of the sea helps define the mundane, such as terrestrial boundaries, but it also provides insight into the dynamic, engulfing, and vulnerable aspects of the marine environment. No single technology provides a complete view of the sea, but by having the foresight to integrate satellite technology with other enabling technologies, several maritime nations are transforming our view of the sea. In so doing, they are providing the intelligence required to appreciate, protect and manage it.

From space we see the magnificent glaciers of the Arctic and Antarctic Ocean. We track the icebergs of the Labrador Sea and North Atlantic, which is the burial ground of the *Titanic*. Where would the *Titanic* be today if its captain had the benefit of satellite and Internet technologies? Ships now sail ice-infested waters routinely, guided by synoptic ice maps that incorporate imagery produced by spaceborne microwave sensors, such as Canada's constellation of Radarsat sensors. During the ice season, such maps are updated several times per week by national ice centers located in Ottawa and Maryland, and delivered to sea via commercial data communications systems.

From space you can see tomorrow's weather, as if you are travelling forward in time. An everlasting memory of living on the shores on Conception Bay, Newfoundland, is looking out my window and seeing a wall of snow sailing across the bay. When it reached my shore, it travelled up the embankment before coating glass that separated me from sea. Eventually, by witnessing this phenomenon, even I could predict how much time I had before weather would sock me into the isolation of our home in St. Philips. There is of course much more to this than minor snow squalls. Certain microwave satellite sensors detect wind itself, specifically its speed and direction. We have measured wind for centuries, but satellites show additional structure and breadth. When these data are composited together, they can show wind patterns across entire oceans. Similar sensors also detect coastal flooding, and when sea level and terrestrial topography data are injected into environmental models, we can estimate flood zones and the extent of flooding with a given set of environmental parameters.

Satellite sensors launched in 1978 became the precursors to a suite of sensors that provide wide-area views of El Niño, which in addition to influencing regional and hemispheric weather patterns also leads to the collapse of the sardine and anchovy fisheries of South America.

From space we can map surface waves. Would Hollywood's fictitious cruise ship *Poseidon* have capsized if its captain had access to an operational wave forecasting system, at the required scales of time and space? It would have warned him when and where to steer his bow into the wave, instead of taking it broadside.

With spaceborne microwave sensors we can measure the overall height of the sea–to centimeter scale. Although the human eye conceives the sea to be flat on a calm day, on large spatial scales it is not, and this physical state leads to large-scale currents. The Gulf Stream is perhaps the best known example of this type of current.

Like most people, I did not know these facts of nature and science when I entered university in Vancouver. I simply viewed the city, English Bay, the Strait of Georgia, and the adjacent Pacific Ocean with my eyes. Like the gardening golfer, what I saw was my personal domain of time and space, as defined by visible energy. The matrix of the sea had yet to present itself. Now that it has, I appreciate Neo's dilemma. With knowledge comes a sense that something needs to be done, but that something seems much larger than any one person can achieve. Like *The Matrix* shipmate who betrayed Neo and his friends, during a dinner of steak and red wine, for some this sense is overwhelming. Some would rather put the knowledge genie back in the bottle, knowing ignorance is indeed bliss. But the next time you flush your toilet, look down and ask which group you belong to.

Every time you flush, ask the same question. It doesn't seem like much and it will not cause the walls of your bathroom to transform into streams of fluorescent code; but eventually, you will see your environment in a different light.

Chapter Four:

The Color of Water

Jacques Cousteau observed the blood of a speared prey flowing the color of emeralds at a depth of one hundred and twenty feet. As the diver swam to the surface, the creature's blood appeared to change color from emerald to brown at fifty-five feet and pink at twenty feet. Only near the surface did its blood flow red. Light behaves differently in water and if you understand this, you will understand much about what you see at sea.

Prior to the twentieth century, the public had little knowledge of what actually lies beneath the sea's surface, other than fish. Until then, our eyes were restricted to surface and shore, with only brief peeks below. This changed with the invention of Jacques Cousteau's famed scuba gear and the proliferation of recreational diving. Technology provided the means to swim through the water column, which is a term oceanographers use when referring to waters at depth. Thus, an oceanographic instrument dropped freely into the sea travels down through the water column until it lands on the seafloor.

As scuba diving evolved and expanded, novelty gave way to reality and both our perception and knowledge of what happens within the water column began to change. A conversation I had in September 2006 with a professional deep-sea diver confirmed this. He was sitting next to me during a flight from New Orleans to Chicago.

The flight took place on the first anniversary of hurricane Katrina. While waiting for my flight I stared at an airport television screen, watching President George W. Bush deliver his speech to surviving residents. As we took off, we caught a glimpse of Air Force One sitting on the tarmac.

Post-Katrina efforts to rebuild the Gulf of Mexico's offshore oil and gas infrastructure had brought the diver to New Orleans. His hard-shell diving helmet, which I saw him stow in the overhead compartment prior to take-off, foretold his profession and provided an easy means to start a conversation.

"Deep-sea diving pays handsomely", he advised, but like others in his profession he travels to wherever he can find work. For this recently divorced family man, home is where his helmet lays. I stared at the tray table in front of me as he spoke of returning to neither house nor apartment, but to a room provided by friends.

"I consider one hundred and twenty feet a shallow-water dive," he said, as he drank his first Heineken. The diver solved the flight attendant's lack of change problem by ordering two beers at once. For a non-diver like me, calling one hundred and twenty feet shallow is like calling Lady Gaga conservative. It is a matter of perspective. What is shocking to some is routine to others. In 1939, Jacques Cousteau witnessed an Arabian sponge diver free dive to one hundred and thirty feet, holding his breath for two and one-half minutes. This is an extremely rare feat that requires conditioning and training. An average recreational skin diver, using goggles and fins, usually goes no deeper than twenty feet or so, and holds their breath for less than a minute.

Cousteau made his first dive to one hundred and thirty feet with an aqualung while diving a Mediterranean wreck in the summer of 1943, the same year he co-invented the scuba tank. In 1955, the same year Rachel Carson published her final marine book, Cousteau and his team of French adventurers were the first to scuba dive off Assumption Island in the Indian Ocean. Then, the waters of Assumption were among Earth's most stunning wonders. They were pristine and home to the grouper fish the team named Ulysses and made famous in their Cannes and Oscar winning film–*The Silent World*. Then, these waters were transparent for two hundred feet!

To see down or up the marine water column for two hundred feet is flabbergasting. It would irrevocably change your perception of the sea. In the temperate waters of North America, one generally sees down anywhere from less than ten to tens of feet, depending on available light and what is on and in the water. As discussed in the previous chapter, run-off from land influences the color and transparency of coastal waters. In populated areas, pollution influences the process and in extreme cases contaminants may prevent a diver from seeing their out-stretched hands. In most cases, however, depth of view is a result of natural processes. Phytoplankton are aquatic plants that live suspended in the water column. They are critical to Rachel Carson's ecosystem approach to environmental management. The greater their concentration the less your depth of view. Usually, phytoplankton cause the water to appear green, but different species of plankton have different effects upon water color. Thus at times they may cause the sea to appear red or brownish. Another natural process, which often dominates when diving near the bottom, is re-suspension of bottom sediments by local currents. A diver's fin, for example, may cause this and thereby reduce visibility to almost nil. Collectively, this knowledge means that Cousteau's 1955 Assumption Island water was extremely low in phytoplankton concentration and not significantly influenced by terrestrial runoff, surface slicks, colored substances, suspended particles or re-suspended sediments. The extreme depth of view of these waters indicates they are not common, but any tourist can attest to the fact that most tropical and sub-tropical waters are relatively clear. As a result, in addition to Jacques Cousteau experiencing these rare waters, the girls of James Bond posed almost naked in the warm, clear, aqua-blue waters of the Caribbean, and Flipper, the bottle-nosed dolphin of twentieth-century television fame, enjoyed the translucent green-blue subtropical waters of Florida.

Unless they are vacationing in such waters, most recreational divers from western countries experience the translucent to opaque and significantly cooler waters of their temperate coasts and impacted shores. Although the beast in the movie *Jaws* was fake, the water seen in this movie, which was shot off Martha's Vineyard, is closer to reality for most westerners than those seen in any James Bond movie.

This is not to suggest that Cousteau only dove in clear conditions. After visiting him on his famed ship *Calypso* in April 1953, for example, James Bond author Ian Fleming referred to the Mediterranean water Cousteau was exploring as opaque and annoyingly so. He likened the experience to driving at dusk, when it is difficult to see but turning your lights on does not help.[16] At the time, Cousteau was exploring a sunken ship, thus the poor visibility may have been due to re-suspension of bottom material and it would have impaired the diving team's ability to work.

The state of the sea has influenced diver performance for as long as the profession has existed. But it also influences the performance of military sensors and weapons. Since the diving glory days of Jacques Cousteau the phrase *diver support* has evolved from supporting underwater film crews, naturalists, and tourists, to supporting national defense, homeland security, and offshore industries. As was the case for underwater breathing equipment during World War II, the military is on the vanguard of our understanding of parameters and processes that influence water transparency and color. Most civilians dive for recreational purposes, to look for marine life, but the navy looks for much more. When a navy diver enters the water he is not looking for souvenirs.

From NATO's perspective, operational oceanography, or rapid environmental assessment in NATO speak, is all about providing deployed forces with environmental information in littoral

---

[16] A. Lycett, *Ian Fleming: The Man Behind James Bond* (Atlanta: Turner, 1995), 242.

waters in tactical time frames and formats. NATO gave birth to this subject in 1995 when its Supreme Allied Commander, Atlantic, identified it as a new requirement. Inaugural NATO orders focused on environmental information pertaining to antisubmarine warfare, amphibious warfare, and mine countermeasures. These requirements soon expanded within NATO and also beyond the military into the civilian applications of homeland and environmental security.

Within western navies, this need for operational environmental information emerged as a result of NATO's post-Cold-War shift in operations towards crisis response and littoral waters. In military speak, the waters in which most operations take place are called the *littoral zone* or simply *the littoral*. Thus, to the navy, Jacques Cousteau engaged in littoral operations. For the military, this involves waters shallow enough to allow the bottom to significantly influence the performance of certain naval sensors. Thus, from the navy's perspective littoral waters extend well out onto a nation's continental shelf, where the water column may be hundreds of meters deep. This differs from the civilian view of the sea, where the word *littoral* is used to describe the inter-tidal zone. Given that Rachel Carson did not go to sea and that she explored the beaches of America's east coast, she personally viewed the sea from a civilian littoral perspective.

Generally, NATO's littoral waters are where phytoplankton grow in their greatest concentrations and therefore influence water transparency and color to their greatest extent. This is why the Oceanographer of the US Navy, which is staffed at the rear-admiral level, is so interested in the biology of the sea. The navy was not very interested in it during World War II, but it is today. The US Navy generates vertical and horizontal diver visibility products routinely, to support its warfighters. It also provides diver visibility products to its allies within NATO. The navy also requires related ocean intelligence products on an operational basis to calibrate and validate marine environmental forecasting models and sensors used to find mines and other objects. In addition to influencing the utility of the diver's eye, water transparency influences the operational range of various electro-optical sensors. Emerging mine hunting sonars, for example, employ laser line scanners for target identification purposes. In coastal waters, lasers are also used from helicopters and aircraft in support of mine countermeasure and amphibious operations.

From a military perspective, operational oceanography is a component of the ocean intelligence sector, which depends upon research for its advancement. As was the case during World War II and the Cold War, when marine research is viewed from a funding perspective, the division between military and civilian research becomes less distinct. Should a civilian scientist make a discovery that has military application, soon thereafter there will be a knock at his or her door, a ring on the phone, a ping in the person's inbox, or a chance encounter at a conference. The caller will not be dressed in black, wear aviator sunglasses or a uniform, or sport a brush cut. But with certainty, they will have research funding.

The Oceanography Society is a civilian science-oriented organization. In 2004, when it was searching for a guest editor for a special publication on optical oceanography in littoral waters, it recruited from the ranks of the US Office of Naval Research (ONR)– just as it had done in 2001, when ONR provided the lead article in the previous special issue on ocean optics. Or consider the 2003 ocean optics issue of the peer-reviewed journal of the American Society for Limnology and Oceanography. It includes articles authored by the who's who of the civilian optical aquatic science community. If you read the fine print of this special issue, you will find the statement: "The publication of this special issue was supported by the US Office of Naval Research–Environmental Optics Program." The years change and so do the civilian science societies, but since the 1940s, the primary driving force for studying the color and transparency of water remains the same. It is not possible to state how much money has been spent on the military component alone, but since the twilight of the Cold War, civilian agencies and the militaries of western countries have spent at least hundreds of millions of dollars developing, building, and utilizing technologies pertaining to the color and transparency of the sea.

When NASA's scientists launched the world's first ocean color satellite sensor, they provided our inaugural view of marine plant biomass at regional, hemispheric, and global scales, thus demonstrating that the base of the marine food chain in the open ocean is not as homogeneous and invariant as once believed. Today, in addition to the United States, the space agencies of several other countries also operate spaceborne ocean color sensors. Their cooperative work supports a network of research programs that aim to quantify the global ocean's contribution to the carbon cycle, as it relates to biological productivity and climate change. Although this pertains to the biology of the sea, these efforts focus on understanding physical mechanisms that drive biological processes and they involve several types of sensors and platforms, not just optical sensors mounted on satellites. By viewing the same environmental event with different types of sensors and platforms, we broaden our understanding of physical, chemical, and biological mechanisms of the sea.

A satellite sensor can detect objects that are less than a meter in size, but this decreases its utility as an environmental monitoring tool. Generally, designing the sensor to detect smaller objects also decreases its field of view. If you are looking for a 155 mm Howitzer gun from space, then you may require sub-meter resolution. But if you are monitoring oceanographic properties, then less than 200 meters, probably between 100 and 200 meters should suffice in nearshore waters.[17] Offshore, where surface waters tend to be more

---

[17] W.P. Bissett et al., "From Meters to Kilometers: A Look at Ocean-Color Scales of Variability, Spatial Coherence, and the Need for Fine-Scale

homogeneous and dominated by larger-scale physical processes, about one kilometer of spatial resolution is usually enough, and allows a viewing width on the order of a few thousand kilometers. This provides the means to view an entire coastal region in a single pass, provided the satellite's orbit is optimal.

An emerging development is to place the ocean-color sensor on a geostationary satellite, as opposed to one that orbits the north and south poles or there about. A geostationary satellite orbits the equator; thus it cannot image high latitudes, such as the Arctic and Southern Oceans. It has the advantage of continuously viewing a fixed area of the sea at whatever repeat time is required. A polar-orbiting satellite can view high latitudes, but it requires days to weeks to review the same location within the Atlantic, Pacific, and Indian Oceans. Within that time frame, a toxic algae bloom can cause regional panic and an enemy can sail an entire fleet into Halifax Harbor.

On 26 June 2010, South Korea launched Goci–the world's first geostationary ocean color sensor. The satellite orbits at the staggering altitude of 36,000 kilometers. By comparison, the international space station flies at about 400 kilometers, which is even lower than polar-orbiting, Earth-observing satellites. Goci images the sea every hour. In addition to increasing the likelihood of detecting the target of interest from a repeat cycle perspective, this rapid repeat time also increases the likelihood of viewing the sea during a cloud-free period and thereby capturing features, targets, and environmental processes that occur on the order of hours to days. Unfortunately, Goci only images waters of the Korean Peninsula.

Another critical issue when observing the color of the sea is that in addition to absorbing and scattering sunlight, certain species of plankton emit their own light through a process called bioluminescence. Witnessing bioluminescence for the first time gave

Remote Sensing in Coastal Ocean Optics," *Oceanography: The Official Magazine of the Oceanography Society* (June 2004), 41.

60

me the same sense of adventure as the first time I saw the Aurora Borealis. When at sea, the best vantage point for witnessing bioluminescence is at the stern because a vessel's motion stimulates the plants to luminesce. At least that is what I thought until a colleague recalled the first time he viewed bioluminescent seawater: "...my personal best view of bioluminescence came as a kid on my father's boat when one night, not wanting to wake everyone by turning on the light, I pumped the head <i.e. toilet> in the dark after doing my business. Imagine my delight as a million little stars lit up the bowl as a sparkling merry go round!... man, I flushed 3-4 times. I woke up my sister, she flushed 2-3 times too."[18]

When you see bioluminescence from the stern of a vessel in the darkness of night, it looks like streams of twinkling miniature lights co-oriented with the ship's wake. This creates the sensation that the boat is cutting through a sea of tiny stars located just below the surface, which lay in darkness until turned on by the arrival of your vessel. If you have yet to witness this, you can get a sense of what it looks like by watching the final scene of the movie *Mamma Mia*, when the nearly newlyweds motor off into a moonlit sea. This scene does not show bioluminescence, but imagine the surface glitter shown in this scene emanating entirely from the launch's bow wave and stern wake and nowhere else, with all the water that lay before the young lovers being dark navy blue.

It is a scene of serenity, unless you are the captain of a submarine stalking the littoral, or a navy diver trying to stay alive. Motor launches sailing idyllically out to sea stimulate bioluminescence, but so can any motion of sufficient force, whether sailing the surface, diving to depth, swimming to shore, or flushing the toilet at sea. Imagine skippering a multi-billion dollar, nuclear-powered attack submarine housing more than 100 sailors into a hostile littoral during a moonless night, thinking you are invisible to

---

[18] Andrew Thomas, University of Maine, personal communication.

the naked eye, only to realize you are lighting up the water around you.

As a result, bioluminescence is one of the subjects studied by the US Office of Naval Research. I am not aware of any navy that has the means to remotely detect bioluminescence on an operational basis over large areas. It requires a sensor that has exceptionally high sensitivity at the required scales of time and space, and can operate at night. Like the human eye, marine electro-optical sensors are designed to detect sunlight, although they also detect incandescent city lights and forest fires at night. South Korea's Goci sensor is an exception, as in addition to daytime detection of sunlight it has a highly-sensitive night-time operational capability, albeit only over specified Asian waters. It is speculative of me to suggest, but given the recent suspected torpedo sinking of a South Korean naval vessel, I doubt South Korea chose this design for purely academic reasons.

Complicating factors are that only certain species of phytoplankton luminesce, some do not require an external force to luminesce, and phytoplankton are not the only marine life to emit their own light. Certain types of bacteria also luminesce, so much so that they turn night seas milky white. The Operational Line Scanner sensors mounted on the US military's constellation of Defense Meteorological Satellite Program satellites observe this phenomenon. This sensor is designed to detect both reflected sunlight and moonlight and operates with high sensitivity. Thus, a satellite constellation known for its weather forecasting application also has potential application to antisubmarine and amphibious warfare operations—no government inefficiency there!

Despite their past limitations, recently launched and future generations of satellite-based sensors hold the key to solving the bioluminescence monitoring problem, at least in part. Like civilian agencies, the military monitors the location of phytoplankton in the sea on a daily basis. When combined with computer-based environmental models that also incorporate data pertaining to physical oceanographic conditions, this knowledge is leading to qualitative estimates of bioluminescence potential in littoral waters. In other words, we do not have the ability to forecast bioluminescence based on actual measurements of it, but we are gaining insight into where and when it is likely to occur. This operational technique of using environmental signatures to detect a target of interest rather than the target itself goes well beyond plankton and bioluminescence. Submerged thermo-nuclear attack submarines, for example, may leave a thermal signature in the sea or create waves detectable from space.

This is leading to the development of what appears to be stunningly simple but very operational ocean intelligence probability products–for example, a map of a given littoral area in which the waters are colored one of three colors: green for go, amber for caution, and red for 'don't say we didn't warn you'. The final decision as to whether to proceed with the operation is up to the commanding warfighter. Although such a map looks like it was colored in a kindergarten class, simplicity is often a reflection of brilliance. Anyone with a Photoshop© license can generate a detailed map that uses the colors of the rainbow and has a multi-megabyte file size, but try sending it out to a submarine over available data communications channels. Then, you will wish you had a really simple file of a few kilobytes.

As simple as it appears, this three-color map is stuffed full of cutting-edge oceanography. If you want to be in the right place at the right time to capture oceanography's next defining moment, then this type of work is the pointy end of your ship, regardless of whether your ultimate goal is a faculty position, inventor of the latest marine gadget, or an operational naval intelligence position.

Unfortunately, existing satellite sensors capable of detecting phytoplankton in the sea have limited ability to differentiate between species of plants, and as already stated, not all species luminesce. A satellite sensor that divides light into much more than the primary colors of the rainbow may hold the key to getting beyond these limitations. Like NASA's inaugurating 1978 ocean color sensor, existing spaceborne sensors divide sunlight into a few bands of energy. When sunlight is divided into dozens to hundreds of bands, we begin to realize that different species of phytoplankton present different spectral signatures within the visible region of the electromagnetic spectrum. If we then design this sensor such that it also senses energy in the near infrared region of the electromagnetic spectrum, then we add the means to account for atmospheric effects. The spectral power of such a sensor is far superior to the human eye and the inaugurating capabilities of the 1970s era sensors.

The type of sensor that is capable of such fine-scale resolution is called a hyperspectral sensor. As brilliant as it was at the time, NASA's inaugural design divided light into five bands, and it did not do a very good job of accounting for atmospheric effects. Even with their few extra bands, advanced sensitivities, and improved atmospheric correction capabilities, the ocean-color sensors that followed this pioneering work only took us so far in our quest to obtain a quantitative view of the sea. Whether you call them subsamples or bands of the electromagnetic spectrum, we have yet to determine how many bands are required to obtain the desired view, or the desired location and width of all required bands.

In the 1960s and 70s, marine adventurers like Jacques Cousteau showed us their new aquatic discoveries on television every week, but not today. As a result, few people realize that the required spaceborne hyperspectral sensor, designed specifically for monitoring littoral waters, was born on 18 September 2009, when a Japanese transfer vessel delivered the HICO sensor to the International Space Station. HICO stands for Hyperspectral Imager for the Coastal Ocean. The sensor's mission includes imaging pre-selected coastal waters at a spatial resolution of about 100 meters. Designed and built by the remote sensing division of the US Naval Research Laboratory, this sensor provides the first real-time, spaceborne hyperspectral monitoring capability of sufficient sensitivity to resolve the marine parameters of interest. One of the first HICO images released to the public is a highly degraded image of waters off the coast of China.[19] That's right, the Russians who share the space station with the west are no longer the perceived threat. But within months of this image being published, a news item came out of Russia advising that Russia has developed its own satellite module for detecting submarines.[20] It is rare for a superpower to even admit they have such sensors, and no reason was provided for making the announcement. Given that the Soviets launched the world's first Earth-orbiting satellite in 1957, no one is suggesting this sensor is Russia's inaugural capability in this area.

Obviously, the Japanese and American navies have their own interests at play here, as they are mandated to do, but there is more to HICO than rapid assessment of the sea in support of the deployed warfighter. NOAA, for example, will use HICO data. Just as certain species of marine plankton luminesce, only certain species are toxic to humans, and this is NOAA territory. These harmful phytoplankton include the infamous red algae and their associated red tides, but they may also present in other dominant colorations. The potentially lethal nature of these plankton was known before Europeans populated the Americas. Government agencies world-wide send technicians into the field to collect and test samples for marine toxicity, but they lack the resources required to adequately sample the marine environment operationally over wide-areas. In addition, it requires a substantial length of time to collect and process a hand-collected field sample for biochemical analyses.

Although funded and built by the military, HICO, its follow-on sensors and forthcoming generations of ocean forecasting models,

---

[19] http://www.ioccg.org/sensors/HICO_summary_for_IOCCG.pdf
[20] P.J. Brown, "US Satellites Shadow China's Submarines," *Asia Times,* May 13, 2010.

will advance this civilian field of health science. Such sensors will also advance other marine fields, such as assessing stocks of harvestable seaweed in intertidal waters and determining the quality of the bottom of certain shallow waters. The latter influences aquaculture, coastal recreation, and nearshore navigation. It also influences amphibious military operations and the performance of sensors used in antisubmarine warfare, but I am getting ahead of myself. In order to achieve such goals, and realize the potential of a research sensor mounted on the International Space Station, we must first understand how light behaves at depth in the sea. There is a very simple means to do this, as demonstrated by Jacques Cousteau and his team mates many decades ago. These French explorers likely witnessed night-time bioluminescence numerous times during their long careers, but as they dove primarily during the day, like everyone else they focused on what they could see with reflected sunlight.

Within three years of developing the aqualung, Cousteau and his team were shooting black and white movies at two hundred and ten feet with natural light in relatively clear tropical and subtropical waters. By 1948, they had discovered that under such conditions they could shoot movies in color at over one hundred feet. At these depths, however, objects do not appear in their actual (i.e. surface) colors due to water's selective absorption and scattering of the different colors of light. This means that a deep-sea diver's view of the sea would be deceptive to the untrained eye.

If you are like me, you have forgotten a good deal of the principles of physics you learned in high school or university. But every time you open your eyes, you see because electromagnetic energy from the sun, or from an artificial source such as a light bulb, illuminates the objects around you. Your physics teacher taught you that this energy travels in waves and that the visible light your eye uses as an energy source does not exist at a single wavelength. It exists within a range of wavelengths. Red light occurs within one part of the range, green within another, and so on. From shortest to longest wavelength, the colors of visible light are violet, blue, green, yellow, orange and red. You may recognize this progression as the colors of a rainbow. I am torturing you with these facts of physics because various wavelengths of optical energy behave differently at depth and if you understand this, you will understand much about what you see at sea.

The longer a color's wavelength, the more its energy is absorbed by seawater and the less it is scattered back to the surface. Thus, the less you see it with your eyes, and the less ocean color sensors see it from space. In other words, this color went into the water but did not come out again, or only some of it came out, and therefore you do not see it or only some of it. Light is energy and this particular unit of energy was absorbed by seawater and converted to heat. You may feel its warmth but you will not witness its color.

Red light is absorbed in the first few feet of water whereas blue light is not. It is scattered down and back to the surface, and because of this, the sea appears blue. Phytoplankton absorb blue light, to a certain extent, and reflect green and because of this seawater containing plankton becomes less blue and increasingly aqua green as their concentration increases. Thus, Jacques Cousteau observed the blood of a speared prey flowing the color of emeralds at a depth of twenty fathoms–one hundred and twenty feet. As the diver swam to the surface, the creature's blood appeared to change color from emerald to brown at fifty-five feet and pink at twenty feet. Only near the surface did its blood flow red. Cousteau benefited from this experience as he subsequently cut himself during an aqualung dive to one hundred and fifty feet. Seeing your blood run green for the first time would cause anxiety in anyone not prepared for it, and panicking at such depth is potentially lethal.

The French explorers went as far as taking colored squares underwater and observing them at various depths. The color red turned pink at fifteen feet and was black at forty. Orange also disappeared at forty feet and at one hundred and twenty feet yellow started to turn green. Cousteau concluded that even in tropical waters, below twenty-five feet, a person only sees about half of the colors in the visible spectrum. They eventually referred to depths of one hundred and fifty feet and beyond as the blue zone. Their observations are approximations, but their experimentation with light, both natural and artificial, are what inspired them to make color movies underwater.

There is more to this than making movies. With quantitative knowledge of the relationship between color and depth, a spaceborne hyperspectral sensor may determine the depth of certain shallow waters from hundreds of miles away, just by observing its color. Very useful if you are not able to measure it on site, which is often the case for military operations.

As discussed previously, however, the sea contains more than water and therefore the color of the sea is not entirely due to the properties of water. Determining depth from color is complex and easy to get wrong. Phytoplankton, bacteria, terrestrial runoff, dissolved molecules, colloidal substances, sediments, and pollutants all cause sea water to deviate from its own color, as do tons of airborne particles of terrestrial origin that blow into the sea every day. Near to shore, especially in tropical and subtropical waters, even the bottom itself may influence what you see from above.

This is how the Yellow Sea got its name. The muddy waters of the Yellow River, which are loaded with suspended, yellow-colored particles, drain into the Yellow Sea and airborne particles of similar source are blown into it. How the Red, Black and White Seas got their names is not as certain. In the case of the Red Sea, bordering mountains and desert contain red-colored minerals and sand, and red-colored bacteria bloom in these waters. But the Red Sea does not usually appear red. Similarly, although heavily polluted and anoxic at depth, the surface waters of the Black Sea are not black.

In the years that followed the dives off Assumption Island, Cousteau and his fellow divers applied their knowledge of light in the sea to advance their skills in cinematography. They also concluded that the practical limit for scuba diving with compressed air was much less than the depths at which my fellow New Orleans-to-Chicago, deep-sea diving airline passenger experienced on a routine basis.

By the time the flight attendant's drinks trolley reached the rear of the plane, the professional diver's second Heineken was on deck, and after describing life on an offshore diving barge to me, I sensed he would agree with my father's view that "a change is as good as a vacation".

"It's like being in a prison that has a great kitchen", the diver said. "But we get paid by the foot and right now I am doing dives to three hundred feet." The diver then described how he could stay down for about fifteen minutes at such depth before having to endure a long decompression process. Boredom is the thought that came to my mind, and Cousteau's account of the French team's first aqualung dive to three hundred feet, in 1947. Cousteau observed that in tropical and subtropical waters, there is usually enough light to work at this depth and beyond. But he also concluded that three hundred feet was the limit for compressed air diving and that two hundred feet was its practical limit. They found that out the hard way. Each paid a physical toll by diving to three hundred feet, and fellow diver Maurice Fargues died by going deeper with the aqualung. Modern deep-sea divers working at such depth do not use compressed air. They use oxygen mixed with other gases.

"That must be hard on the body", I said, while eating my in-flight cookie. "It must be a young man's profession."

"I'm forty-three," the diver replied, as he finished his last beer for the flight, "and that is not unusual in my profession. Most of the guys coming out of dive school do not stick with it. Once they start, they find it is not what they thought it would be. It's not all about clear water and swimming with dolphins."

Chapter Five:

Rule the Waves

Everyone is aware of World War II, but few people credit oceanographers for saving us from a third.

During World War II and the Cold War that followed, Rachel Carson's beloved marine science community was pressed into military service. Like Jacques Cousteau and my father, scientists were enticed by naval funding and an underlying desire to serve one's country. As a result, while the public continued to view the sea as a biological wonder, source of food, and means of transportation, marine science transformed its primary focus from biology to the navy-oriented subjects of physics and geophysics. No one rules the sea, but this symbiotic relationship between science and war helped redefine bragging rights over who rules the waves. It also changed the definition of *oceanography*.

Prior to World War II, oceanography encompassed all science of the sea.[21] By such definition, a biologist studying the anatomy of marine fish in a laboratory could also be called an oceanographer. It was also ill-defined, to the extent that in 1936, after three hours of discussion, the faculty of the Scripps Institution of Oceanography could not agree on its definition.[22]

During and after World War II, the Soviet Union and the United States realized the relationship between oceanographic

---

[21] H.Stommel, *Science of the Seven Seas* (New York, Cornell Maritime Press), 23.
[22] W. Munk, "Harald U. Sverdrup and the War Years," *Oceanography: The Official Magazine of the Oceanography Society* (December 2002), 12.

knowledge and global naval supremacy, and capitalized upon it–so much so that by the end of the 1960s, the two countries accounted for approximately seventy percent of the world's oceanographic capability.[23] Previously dominant countries in the field, including Norway, Sweden, Great Britain, and Germany, could not match the marine science budgets of these emerging superpowers.

Essentially, the navies of the Soviet Union and the United States shanghaied the marine science agenda. By the time I entered graduate school in the late 1970s, their efforts had redefined oceanography as the study of the dynamics of the marine environment. Focus had shifted from the intuitive to the strategic, from descriptive biology to mathematical explanations of the dynamics of the sea.

The naval influence was so great that our present view of the sea would not exist if World War II and the Cold War had not occurred. In order to rule the waves, a superpower needs to know how the ocean functions. Supremacy requires knowledge, including the ability to forecast the sea's behavior. The invasion of Normandy, for example, benefited from wave forecasting techniques developed co-operatively by the United States and Great Britain during World War II. During the Cold War the primary oceanographic focus was on antisubmarine warfare, which requires understanding of the behavior of sound in water (i.e. acoustics). This in turn requires precise knowledge of the structure and dynamics of the sea as well as accurate databases of water temperature, bathymetry, and the topography and quality of the sea floor. These requirements translated into a focus on physical, geophysical, and physicochemical aspects of the sea.

The timing of this transition depends upon where you live and which aspect of the field dominates your view. The

---

[23] E. Wenk Jr., *The Politics of the Ocean* (Seattle: University of Washington Press, 1972), 232.

oceanographer Carl Wunsch, for example, pegs the birth of dynamical oceanography in the United States to a paper published by Henry Stommel in 1948, on the westward intensification of wind-driven currents. This definitive paper unlocked the mystery of western-boundary currents, such as the Gulf Stream, and set the stage for future advancements in physical oceanography. But the field itself is decades older. It started in Scandinavia. Even within the United States, Edward H. Smith's 1926 guide on how to determine ocean currents demonstrates the Scandinavian approach had reached North America prior to World War II.

Descriptive views of wind-driven and deep-sea currents began to gel in Europe during the late nineteenth century, but much of the advancement was qualitative (i.e. descriptive; not explained mathematically). Although "very sophisticated mathematical physics" existed in Europe during this period, it was not applied to prevailing hypotheses on ocean dynamics.[24] Europe's leading physicists of the day were not interested in the dynamics of the sea and the leading navies had yet to realize the relationship between physical oceanography and naval supremacy, because physical oceanography as we know it today did not exist then.

The transition was more of a "subtle shift"[25] The mathematical approach to ocean dynamics was born around the turn of the century when Scandinavian physicists and mathematicians applied themselves to the subject.[26] The historian Eric L. Mills credits the Norwegian meteorologist Henrik Mohn with the first dynamic analysis of ocean circulation, in the mid to late 1880s, and concludes another Norwegian physicist, Vilhelm Bjerknes, gave birth to

---

[24] E.L. Mills, *The Fluid Envelope of Our Planet: How the Study of Ocean Currents Became a Science* (Toronto: University of Toronto Press, 2009), 77.
[25] Ibid., 192.
[26] Mills, *The Fluid Envelope of Our Planet*; Munk, "The Evolution of Physical Oceanography in the Last Hundred Years," 135.

mathematical physical oceanography a few years thereafter.[27] In Mills' view of the sea, both dynamical meteorology and dynamical oceanography originated with Bjerknes and flourished in Scandinavia and Germany for years thereafter in the hands of renowned disciples and followers.

North American marine scientists were slow to adopt these Scandinavian techniques as were the navies of western countries. The Scripps Institution of Oceanography in California and Woods Hole Oceanographic Institution in Massachusetts, America's dominating oceanographic schools during World War II, started prior to the war as marine biological research laboratories. Canada also founded marine biological research stations in the early 1900s, one in St. Andrews, New Brunswick and another in Nanaimo, British Columbia, where they remain as such. Initially, Scripps and Woods Hole were largely funded by private donations whereas their Canadian equivalents were publicly funded. Scripps got its name from the wealthy family that funded much of its early development, and the Rockefeller Foundation financed the launch of Woods Hole.

Both Scripps and Woods Hole emerged prior to extinction of the gentleman scientist, who pursued science for the love of science without the distraction of having to formulate research programs to meet the objectives of public funding. Columbus Iselin, for example, was the son of a wealthy New York banker and the nephew of a four-time defender of America's Cup. In the 1920s, when he was in his twenties, Iselin self-financed research in the North Atlantic Ocean, including the cost of his seventy-seven foot schooner *Chance* and its crew. He was among the first to delineate characteristics of the Labrador Current, which by that time was a hot spot of oceanographic research, largely as a result of the sinking of the *Titanic*. Alexander Agassiz, the famed ichthyologist also self-financed his early work and sometime during this period was accompanied by the American

---

[27] Mills, *The Fluid Envelope of Our Planet*, 91, 95, 104.

marine biologist Henry Bigelow. According to Henry Stommel, it was Bigelow who encouraged Columbus Iselin to get into oceanography. Bigelow also mentored Rachel Carson.

Publicly-funded Canadian facilities focused their research programs on the biology of fish well into the twentieth century, even as other nations sent physical scientists off its coasts. On 14 April 1912, the White Star liner RMS *Titanic* sank off the Grand Banks of Newfoundland. The British were the first on the scene to do follow-up physical oceanographic work, followed quickly by the Americans.[28] In addition to the *Titanic* being British, at the time Newfoundland was still in British hands. The meeting these two nations held in London the following year was the prelude to the 1914 International Convention for the Safety of Life at Sea (SOLAS). This led to formation of an International Ice Patrol of the shipping lanes of the North Atlantic. The US Coast Guard took the lead on this. The officer they appointed to head up related physical oceanography was the aforementioned Edward H. Smith. He did his masters and doctorate degrees under Henry Bigelow but studied physical oceanography under the renowned Norwegian oceanographer, Bjørn Helland-Hansen, a disciple of Vilhelm Bjerknes. Canada's research focus on marine biology was of little interest to the Ice Patrol and coast guards of the day. Even in the 1920s, Canadian efforts continued to founder partly because they lacked a physical oceanography focus and therefore lacked a physical oceanographer.[29] Given that the Canadian navy was born in 1910, this is understandable but its effect was felt for decades thereafter. The University of British Columbia did not establish Canada's first oceanography department until thirty-seven years after the sinking of the *Titanic*. Canada's only west-coast

---

[28] E.L. Mills, "Canadian Marine Science from Before *Titanic* to BIO," in *Voyage of Discovery: Fifty Years of Marine Research at Canada's Bedford Institute of Oceanography,* ed. M. Latremouille, (in preparation 2012), 9.
[29] Ibid., 9.

physical oceanographer during World War II, J.P. Tully, had ties to the Royal Canadian Navy and US Navy as they shared his interests in the physical oceanography of the Northwest Pacific Ocean. Tully spent the war working on Canada's antisubmarine warfare efforts.

The US Navy was well established by the turn of the century and by the 1920s it had more men and women in uniform than the Royal Navy. When World War II struck Europe, the US Navy was well positioned to influence the field of marine science. Scripps Institution for Biological Research in La Jolla, California, evolved into Scripps Institution of Oceanography in 1923, and Massachusetts' Woods Hole facility became Woods Hole Oceanographic Institution in 1930. Both institutions maintain strong biological components to this day, but about the time of World War II, their primary focus changed from marine biology to marine acoustics, geophysics, and physical oceanography. The US Navy financed much of this transition, with such influence that it shifted the epicenter of western oceanography to the United States. It began, however, with a transitioning of knowledge from Scandinavia to the United States. On the east coast this can be traced to the aforementioned 1926 publication by Edward H. Smith, which he conceived and drafted while in Norway the previous year. On the west coast, it started with George McEwen and his application of Scandinavian techniques, but it did not take root until Harald Sverdrup, a Norwegian and former student and assistant of Vilhelm Bjerknes, was appointed director of California's Scripps Institution of Oceanography in 1936, just three years prior to the outbreak of war. If you search for a marine science example of someone being in the right place at the right time, resulting in major personal accomplishments, this is it. An east coast example is Henry Stommel's post-World War II and Cold War accomplishments while he was at Woods Hole, which was also Rachel Carson's beloved research facility during the same period.

Henry Bigelow was the founding director of Woods Hole, but during World War II it was directed by the aforementioned Columbus

Iselin. With navy funding, Iselin's privileged connections, and pioneering physical and geophysical scientists on staff, the institute prospered and expanded, from a staff of ninety three to three hundred and thirty five. Iselin became one of Woods Hole's most influential directors. His portrait graced the cover of the 6 July 1959 issue of *Time* magazine. Prosperity continued at Woods Hole after Iselin's tenure, with directors such as Paul Fye, who took over in 1958 and was an avid supporter of navy-focused research and development.

The Swedish-born physicist Carl-Gustaf Rossby left Woods Hole in 1940 to become the chair of the newly formed Institute of Meteorology at the University of Chicago. There, he continued to aid the Allied war effort while becoming one of the world's most recognized meteorology and oceanography scientists. Rossby's portrait appeared on the cover of the 17 December 1956 edition of *Time* magazine.

Similarly, Maurice Ewing spent the war years at Woods Hole, working cooperatively with the marine physicist J. Lamar Worzel and others. During World War II, Worzel's research in marine acoustics and geophysics helped guide US Navy operational procedures for antisubmarine warfare. In 1949, Ewing left Woods Hole to become the first director of the newly formed Lamont Geological Observatory in New York, which today is known as the Lamont-Doherty Earth Observatory. Within a decade, it joined the ranks of the country's leading marine research organizations.

Roger Revelle joined Scripps in the 1930s as a graduate student. During World War II he served in the US Navy as commander of the oceanographic section of the Bureau of Ships. He became director of Scripps in 1951, during the Cold War. In addition to managing the institution itself, he became one of the first to study and report on global warming and he helped develop key international oceanographic programs.

Everyone is aware of World War II, but few people credit oceanographers for saving us from a third. Roger Revelle does, and he was well positioned to comment upon it. While at Scripps, Revelle influenced US Navy funding and was in charge of several US Navy-backed oceanographic field programs in the Pacific Ocean. He believed oceanographers helped prevent a third world war by helping the US Navy develop the means to launch nuclear missiles from its *Polaris* submarines, as a deterrent against nuclear attack by the Soviets.[30] After World War II, the United States recognized the possibility of nuclear warheads being placed on Soviet attack submarines, thereby providing a covert means to attack the United States from its shores. This invigorated that country's submarine and antisubmarine warfare programs.

In 1940, Walter Munk became a graduate student of Harald Sverdrup, who ran Scripps until 1948. Starting in 1942, Walter Munk and Harald Sverdrup worked on a navy-backed wave prediction for Allied landings project. Munk was also a familiar face at Woods Hole after the war. According to Walter Munk, when developing the *Time* magazine cover that featured Columbus Iselin, staff also prepared an article on Roger Revelle, making the decision as to cover choice "at the last minute",[31] Thus, while a wealthy gentleman scientist garnered public profile, a silently-distinguished navy man stood in his shadow.

Not all of the physical and geophysical scientists at Scripps and Woods Hole agreed with this military-funded focus. Henry Stommel is said to have left Ewing's group shortly after arriving at Woods Hole in 1944, and he opposed Fye's preferred naval orientation. He went on to become a legend in his field. Upon his death in 1992, *The New York Times* described him as "one of the most

---

[30] J.D. Hamblin, *Oceanographers and the Cold War* (Seattle: University of Washington Press, 2005), 261.
[31] W. Munk and D.Day, "Glimpses of Oceanography in the Postwar Period," *Oceanography: The Official Magazine of the Oceanography Society* (September 2008).

influential oceanographers of his time."[32] Another Woods Hole physical oceanographer, William von Arx, also openly opposed politically-motivated science programs, but such efforts fought the proverbial losing battle. Von Arx participated in navy-backed research in the Pacific Ocean and Stommel dedicated his 1945 book *Science of the Seven Seas* to "the members of the US Navy V-12 Unit at Pierson College".

In the nonsensical tale of *The Hitchhiker's Guide to the Galaxy*, mice commission aliens to build planet Earth, for experimental purposes. Slartibartfast, one of the commissioned designers, subsequently wins an award for designing the fjords of Norway. Perhaps it is the history of oceanography that causes this tidbit of fiction to stand out for me. Although Slartibartfast believed his name was not important, his efforts were profound from an oceanographic perspective. Throughout the twentieth century the United States ruled the western waves, but the crinkly edges of this accomplishment were courtesy of Norway, at least during the design stage.

---

[32] W. Sullivan, "Henry Stommel, 71, Theoretician Influential in Ocean Current Study," *New York Times,* January 21, 1992.

Chapter Six:

Sputnik Changes Our View

Many scientists bristle at the suggestion that they focus their work on projects that have political objectives. It is a matter of what makes a scientist a scientist, but also of who gets to formulate and control the projects. It is a matter of autonomy. Regardless, the US did not drive this great expansion in marine science to fulfill academic objectives.

The Soviet Union's shocking October 1957 launch of *Sputnik*, the world's first Earth-orbiting satellite, awoke the West to the fact that the Soviet Union had gained technical superiority in an area critical to national security. In the United States, this invigorated science funding. When *Sputnik* was launched, the US National Science Foundation had a budget of $53 million. Two years later it had almost tripled to $138 million.[33] The launch also reoriented US marine science policy such that the initial post–World War II emphasis on cooperation with eastern and developing countries diminished in favor of competing against the Soviets.

In 1959, the United States also bankrolled NATO's new undersea research center in La Spezia, Italy. It became a focal point for allied oceanography, especially with respect to antisubmarine warfare. Today, this research center is recognized as the birth place of NATO's rapid environmental assessment program. Initially, this program focused on providing meteorology and oceanography products in support of antisubmarine warfare, mine countermeasures, and amphibious warfare. These applications of oceanography are the

---

[33] Hamblin, *Oceanographers and the Cold War*, 94.

same applications that dominated the field during the navy days of Jacques Cousteau, Ian Fleming, and my father. Jacques Cousteau, for example, received his inaugural research funding from the French navy with the objective of clearing German mines. These three military applications are the reason why oceanographic institutions in the United States were funded to expand their research programs. But instead of being funded to develop scuba technologies, these institutions worked on marine acoustics, geophysics and meteorology. In comparison, the level of funding received by Jacques Cousteau was tiny.

By the late 1950s to early 1960s, oceanography was such a popular topic in Washington that two House of Representative Committees vied for its jurisdiction.[34] Oceanographers were held in such esteem that their faces graced the cover of *Time* magazine. Even Jacques Cousteau made the cover of *Time* during this period.[35] The popularity of the subject reached a level where the primary problem was not funding but coordinating a national program.

Other NATO countries also re-prioritized their marine science programs during the Cold War. The United States dominated, to a point of overshadowing, but it was not alone. To this day, for example, the Canadian navy has more acoustics specialists in uniform than oceanographers.

Although Canada is recognized for its contributions to oceanographic congresses held in the 1920s and 30s,[36] key university faculty members were brought in from the United States and United Kingdom in the late 1960s and early 70s. Renowned in their respective professional disciplines, they had little or no connection with Canada and its youth. They did, however, know oceanographic

---

[34] Ibid., 148.

[35] Jacques Cousteau was featured in the 28 March 1960 issue of *Time* magazine.

[36] Hamblin, *Oceanographers and the Cold War*, 5.

techniques developed with US Navy funding and sought after by allied navies. This approach was necessary due to a paucity of oceanographers in Canada at the time, particularly physical oceanographers. Also, diversifying departmental faculty with foreign scientists is an established graduate school procedure. It builds a well-rounded and internationally influential faculty. In this particular case, it provided Canada with immediate connections to the formidable US oceanographic community.

In the late 1960s, for example, Gordon A. Riley was brought in from Yale University to head the new department of oceanography at Dalhousie University, in Nova Scotia. In addition to his renowned academic experience, Riley was a member of the influential US National Academy of Sciences Committee on Oceanography, whose 1959 report inextricably linked the subjects of oceanography and national security, with emphasis upon physical oceanography.

I was a research associate at Dalhousie's department of oceanography when the department assigned me Riley's vacated office in 1986. He died the year before, while he was professor emeritus within the department. Faculty members and surviving family had been through his office and removed whatever they felt was important. I was told I could have whatever remained. From my perspective, it stood much as he left it, with his ashtray still on the desk and his bookshelves filled with testaments to the post-war rebirth of oceanography. In the months that followed, I leafed through volume upon volume. Some were the inaugural volumes of what became a renowned journal.

During my graduate student days, I had passed Gordon Riley in the hallways on occasion, with amiable nods and smiles, but by then he was not directly involved in the day to day research of new grad students. It was not until I inhabited his vacated office that I began to realize his role in the formation of my profession. Only now do I appreciate how much he influenced my view of the sea. Although Gordon Riley did not sit on my research committee, he and my PhD thesis supervisor, P.J. Wangersky, were like professional brothers, having gone through the heyday of oceanography together during their time at Yale University. But Riley was senior to Wangersky, with the former being a member of the graduate research committee of the latter.

Gordon Riley was Yale's first professor of oceanography and lists the likes of Columbus Iselin and Maurice Ewing as his "two oldest and best friends."[37] He co-published with Stommel and Munk, worked in the Pacific with Revelle and in the Atlantic with von Arx. Only now do I realize Gordon Riley was among those who defined the word *oceanography*, as it is known today.

I shared my days at Dalhousie University with founders of the field and their graduate students who became university professors. Biological oceanography Professor Eric Mills, for example, arrived about the time of Wangersky. They were not the only next generation American marine scientists to join Riley in Canada, and not all were from biology, or American per se.

Gordon Riley did it the hard way, though. He was a marine biologist when the US joined World War II, not a physicist or geophysicist. The US Navy's thirst for oceanographic knowledge was so great at the time that even biologists were recruited into its world of ocean intelligence. In Riley's case, he was first assigned to studies of anti-fouling paints, reportedly for ship's hulls. Presumably, his work was also applicable to other objects, such as the housings of sensors and mines. Eventually, he led navy-backed physical oceanography projects in the Pacific, having taught himself physical oceanography by teaming with leading marine physicists of the day while consuming their literature and the recognized 1942 treatise *The Oceans*, written by the aforementioned Norwegian oceanographer

---

[37] G.A. Riley, "Reminiscences of an Oceanographer," Unpublished manuscript, Department of Oceanography, Dalhousie University (NS), 106.

Harald Sverdrup, along with two co-authors from Scripps Institution of Oceanography–Johnson and Fleming.

His time on the west coast of the United States, at Scripps, likely had significant impact on the development of oceanography in Canada. When Riley inaugurated the oceanography department at Dalhousie, he implemented the approach first developed at Scripps, whereby the student studies all four sub-disciplines of oceanography before specializing in one.

Riley arrived in Canada when it was also opening its newest federal marine research institution–the Bedford Institute of Oceanography. It is located just down the road from the Canadian Forces' marine defense research agency–DRDC Atlantic. During the decades that followed Riley's arrival and the Institute's inauguration, Dalhousie educated Canada's future east-coast oceanographers. The Bedford Institute took them to sea to conduct their research and then either hired them upon graduation or watched the navy lure them into the classified world of ocean intelligence. Many graduates who stayed in Halifax chose to do neither, and instead helped to launch what has become one of the largest concentrations of marine technology companies in the world. Although only about 400,000 people live in Halifax, eighty ocean technology companies are located within its city limits. The British founded the city and took it to war, twice, but the Americans played the lead role in educating and establishing its oceanographic community.

While occupying Gordon Riley's office, I found his copy of what became the oceanographer's successor to *The Oceans*. Published between 1962 and 1963, the three volumes of *The Sea* were written by a multitude of leading edge World War II and Cold War era oceanographers, including Iselin, Revelle, Ewing, Munk, Riley, and von Arx, among others. From a physical and geophysical perspective, they updated and superseded its predecessor. According to the preface to these works, Roger Revelle, the shadow navy-man from Scripps Institution of Oceanography, suggested they be written. This preface

also documents the field's transition from a primarily marine biology to a marine physics, geochemical, and geophysics focus:
"It was also apparent that we could do no more than include biology in so far as it was directly related to physical, chemical and geological processes in the ocean and on the ocean floor."

Thus, if it is relevant to parameters and processes of interest to Allied navies, then we include it. *The Sea* did address topics pertaining to the emerging field of biological oceanography, but not the fading field of marine biology.

Throughout the 1960s, when the public profiles of Jacques Cousteau, Ian Fleming and Rachel Carson peaked, and the Cold War was at full throttle, in addition to these scientific discoveries, the United States experienced a renaissance in marine science policy, technology and surveying that encompassed more than military objectives. This was accomplished first through the presidency of John F. Kennedy, then Lyndon B. Johnson and finally Richard Nixon, who in July 1970 announced the formation of the National Oceanic and Atmospheric Administration (NOAA).

During this period, the US Navy continued to dominate expenditures in the oceanographic research and marine mapping sectors, but as a decreasing percentage of overall sector expenditures. In 1961-62, for example, the oceanographic budget estimate for the Department of Defense nearly doubled whereas the Department of Commerce's nearly tripled.[38] From 1960 to 1966, the United States launched twenty new ships, doubled the number of scientists in the field, and tripled the number of students.[39]

Edward Wenk Jr. was the first executive secretary of the US Marine Sciences Council and therefore a Washington insider at the time. According to Wenk, the United States experienced a reawakening in the marine sector because knowledge of the sea "was

---

[38] Hamblin, *Oceanographers and the Cold War*, 155.
[39] Wenk, *The Politics of the Ocean*, 95.

so deficient as to merit government intervention."[40] Jacques Cousteau's scuba sea expanded our frontiers and captured our imaginations, and the girls of James Bond stimulated the fantasies of adolescent and adult males, but they did not expand our knowledge of the dynamics of the sea. They presented a descriptive view but not the newly-defined oceanographic view. We could see the sea, but the scuba view did not understand the forces that defined it. Roger Revelle summarized the situation simply by stating, "We tend to look at the ocean rather than ask questions of it."[41]

At this point, the three forces of public opinion, science, and national defense harmonized to change the way we view the sea. It was an unwitting axis of enlightenment. The United States wove its national security policy with a desire to consider the social consequences of marine science, and then strapped the lot on the back of public opinion. The taxpayer took care of it from there.

The American public supported massive expansion in marine science even though it was not aware of certain navy-funded oceanographic programs. This ignorance was not due to lack of interest. After all, more than a million copies of Rachel Carson's *The Sea Around Us* were in public circulation. Rather, this ignorance was due to the fact that much of this science was and remains classified.[42]

Navy-funded physical and geophysical oceanographic research conducted during the Cold War produced volumes of hydrographic data, but most of this pioneering work was withheld from the open literature for some fifteen years. In hindsight, this secrecy probably contributed to the public's prolonged ignorance of what oceanography was actually about during the Cold War, and thus

---

[40] Ibid., 401.

[41] R.R. Revelle, 1956. *Deep Sea Research as a Cooperative Enterprise*, RRP, AC 6A, Box 63, Folder 16. Re-quoted from Hamblin, *Oceanographers and the Cold War*, 76.

[42] Munk and Day, "Glimpses of Oceanography in the Postwar Period," 15.

to the public's prolonged focus on marine biology years after this subject ceased to drive marine science.

The distribution clamps put on this information caused discontent among scientists. It created a class of privileged oceanographers who as a result of their security clearances had access to advanced hydrographic charts, ships, and international research programs. They were, however, unhappy about the situation. Scientists must publish in their respective peer-reviewed journals or watch their career stagnate.

The classification issue did not boil into public view because it was not a battle between the navy and the oceanographic community. The decision to classify this information was made jointly by navy personnel and participating civilian oceanographers who cared about issues pertinent to the US Navy. It was a unique arrangement in which the navy gave scientists freedom to choose among research subjects of interest. The field was no longer the realm of gentlemen scientists, but those who participated had access to significant funding.

One day in 1959, this unwitting axis presented a rare display to the international media–both eastern and western. It happened during Jacques Cousteau's famed maiden *Calypso* voyage to New York City. To the international press assembled at New York's harbor front to cover the First International Congress of Oceanography, the sight of Cousteau serving wine on *Calypso's* deck while his laundry hung drying in the wind must have been a photo-op *extraordinaire*. But how many photographers were permitted to photograph the Soviet oceanographic research vessel *Mikhail Lomonosov*, which was docked alongside with an armed guard standing at the foot of its gangway? How many noticed the US oceanographers who showed up to talk shop with Soviet acoustic/antisubmarine warfare specialists, who had sailed into New York on board the *Lomonosov*?[43]

---

[43] Ibid., 17.

Whether it be in support of naval supremacy, homeland security, fisheries, aquaculture, third-world development, climate change or definition of sovereign boundaries, since the demise of the gentleman scientist, marine science has sailed on the winds of one public policy or another. Many scientists bristle at the suggestion that they focus their work on projects that have political objectives. It is a matter of what makes a scientist a scientist, but also of who gets to formulate and control the projects. It is a matter of autonomy. Regardless, the US did not drive this great expansion in marine science to fulfill academic objectives. According to the historian Jacob Hamblin, Edward Wenk Jr. played a key role in the government's abandonment of the scientist's point of view.[44]

Understanding physical and geophysical processes that drive the ocean is critical to naval operations, and during the Cold War the navy knew more than the general population. But given the fact that the ocean remains a scientific frontier to this day, it is certain that during this period even the navies of NATO and the Soviet Union had a hunger for greater knowledge of the dynamics of the marine environment. I am uncertain as to who brought this knowledge deficiency to the attention of US policy makers, but some believe the US Navy's Chief of Naval Research initiated it in 1956. While sitting on a sea chest of classified oceanographic knowledge and underwater technologies, he wrote a letter to the US National Academy of Sciences, which eventually resulted in the formation of the National Academy of Science's Committee on Oceanography.[45]

The committee's 1959 report, published approximately two years after the launch of *Sputnik*, clearly links the subject of oceanography to national defense, with profound statements such as a doubling of the navy's effectiveness with the ability to forecast marine environmental parameters that influence practically every weapon

---

[44] Hamblin, *Oceanographers and the Cold War*, 241.
[45] Wenk, *The Politics of the Ocean*, 39.

used by the navy.[46] The report emphasized the physical and geophysical aspects of the field, recognizing their relevance to specific naval operations, such as antisubmarine warfare.

Eventually, President Johnson appointed a highly influential commission to formulate national marine policy. Established in 1967, it had fifteen members of which only two were representatives of marine academia. The person in charge of the commission, Julius A. Stratton, was chairman of the Ford Foundation and an electrical engineer by profession. There were as many lawyers and economists on the commission as scientists. Other members came from industry and the public service. This included a representative of the oil industry as even in the 1960s offshore oil deposits were recognized for their potential benefits to the United States.

The Stratton Commission is best known for its conception of NOAA and for passing this idea on to the president in its final report. Today, this agency is North America's leading civilian meteorology and oceanography agency. Without in situ and spaceborne sensors operated by NOAA, for example, Canada would have difficulty tracking and forecasting subtropical storms and hurricanes that approach its east coast over southern waters.

The New York Times does not comment on the science of oceanography very often, but in 1969 it editorialized on the findings of the Stratton Commission. The editorial found the commission's work to be priceless and "a rare combination of imagination and realism..." According to this and one other *New York Times* article on the Stratton report, the perception of oceanography in 1969 was one of adventure, economics, security, and quality of life in coastal cities. In this Stratton view, "seasteading" would replace homesteading, and underwater tourism would compete with foreign travel.

The prevailing perspective also provided insight into how lacking the unclassified view of the sea was during this period. The

---

[46] Hamblin, *Oceanographers and the Cold War*, 144.

editorial notes, for example, the Stratton Commission's view that we could avoid hazards associated with nuclear power plants by building these plants in the sea, and that in the decades that follow the 1960s we would be able to change the environment to better meet our needs. Fortunately, deep-sea circulation hypotheses presented by Henry Stommel and others put the brakes on dumping radioactive wastes in the sea, and marine academics sitting on the Stratton Commission did influence the commission's final report. It also provided, for example, a detailed plan for advancing scientific knowledge. Thus, although knowledge of the sea continued to be fragmented, when President Nixon approved the formation of NOAA in 1970, public perception had begun to evolve such that we at least understood the overarching role of the sea. As summarized perceptively by Nixon, when announcing the formation of NOAA:

"The oceans and the atmosphere are interacting parts of the total environmental system upon which we depend not only for the quality of our lives, but for life itself."[47]

This poetic quotation stands out because it reminds me of the poetic pen and ecosystem approach of Rachel Carson, who died just before the creation of the Stratton Commission. During this period, Carson convinced the public that we can change the environment, as subsequently recommended by the Stratton Commission, but Carson demonstrated we are undermining life on Earth, not improving it.

By the time the Stratton report was released to the public in 1969, US marine science programs were influenced by scientists but driven by public policy. The marine science community had gained a substantial source of public funding but had lost the lottery of public opinion. The gentleman scientist had retired and his replacement

---

[47] The president's message to the Congress of the United States of America, 9 July 1970, pertaining to Reorganization Plans No. 3 and No. 4, outlining the establishment of the Environmental Protection Agency and the National Oceanic and Atmospheric Administration (NOAA).

started to lose public reverence. Even international marine science initiatives changed, such that their objectives and structure were determined by public servants working on a government to government level, not by practicing scientists working on a scientist to scientist level, which was the case immediately after World War II.

The science community's intentional linking of research funding to military objectives was so successful that scientists unwittingly surrendered control of the science agenda to bureaucrats and diplomats. National and international science programs became the deliverable rather than a means to a scientific objective. Eventually, the scientists that worked on them, often the most renowned of their discipline, awoke to find themselves enslaved in program administration and employee supervision. In 1978, for example, Henry Stommel abruptly resigned from such programs and refused to serve on related committees.

The marine science community's inability to publicize some of its most exciting discoveries likely contributed to this situation. As a result of this navy-funded research, marine geophysicists secretly advanced understanding of the formation and dynamics of planet Earth. Today, such information is referenced under the subject of plate tectonics. Physical oceanographers also secretly detected mesoscale eddies for the first time, which previously went undetected due to inadequate sampling, even though such eddies contain more than ninety percent of the kinetic energy of the ocean.

Stommel's self-inflicted exorcism from the distractions of bureaucracy is easy to understand when one considers the rewards of scientific discovery. To appreciate just one of the exciting military applications of hydrographic and geophysical databases created during the Cold War, watch the Cold War themed movie *The Hunt for Red October*–particularly the scene where the captain of a Russian nuclear-powered attack submarine attempts to evade detection by blindly throttling the massive sub between narrowly-spaced seafloor canyons, just meters above the seafloor, with nothing more than a stopwatch in hand and precise knowledge of vessel speed, bottom currents and seafloor topography. In my mind, this ranks among the best of Hollywood's modern naval scenes. Cold War era oceanographic cruises likely lacked such bravado, but not the excitement, and I get a chuckle out of the fact that the sub's captain is played by Sean Connery, who also played James Bond in the 1960s.

I doubt the producers intended their movie to be viewed from this academic perspective, but in my personal view of the sea, the Cold War was the heyday of oceanography. Massive growth in research funding, an urgent sense of national security stemming from fear of nuclear annihilation, public reverence of outstanding scientists, and secretive but pioneering discoveries support this view. But the US Navy's need for secrecy eventually caused the civilian oceanographic and naval acoustic communities to go their separate ways. Something was lost with this passing to maturity. During a 2008 assembly of The Oceanography Society (TOS), Walter Munk closed his presentation with a question:
"When TOS meets again in 2028 to celebrate another 20 years, will we have recovered some of the excitement and joy of the postwar period?"[48]

It is the age of terrorism, but not of world war or nuclear annihilation. It is the age of global warming and perhaps irrevocable environmental change. It is the age of national sovereignty, when nations maneuver to lay claim to the final frontiers of planet Earth– the Arctic and Antarctica. Global terrorism, global warming, environmental annihilation, global ownership–the sea features in all. Yet, one of America's pre-eminent physical oceanographers does not feel the excitement of former days, and I sense he is not alone in this view.

In the late 1950s and early 60s, science budgets doubled and tripled in the United States. Since 1979, ocean science funding has

---

[48] Munk and Day, "Glimpses of Oceanography in the Postwar Period," 21.

fallen from 7 to 3.5 percent of the federal research budget.[49] Growth creates new opportunities, results in new discoveries, and generates a concomitant sense of accomplishment. Shrinking budgets generate the stressful sense of having to do more with less. Even without crass consideration of money, although we have a new set of pressing needs and a buffet of emerging ocean-observing technologies, we have yet to link the two in a manner that inspires the general public. People are inspired by the applications and the people who invent them, not the underlying technology. The aqualung, for example, did not in its own right inspire the masses or even Allied Command when the French invented it in the early 1940s. It was Cousteau's groundbreaking applications that led to the late twentieth-century view of the subsea. The public awaits the next inspirational view. It awaits the next Carson or Cousteau. Until then, the field continues to percolate along, creating and cataloging a smorgasbord of technologies and facts until someone figures out how to marry the two within the public domain. Meanwhile, what is happening within the classified view is anyone's guess, but I speculate it will play a hand in our next great view of the sea.

---

[49] U.S. Commission on Ocean Policy, *An Ocean Blueprint for the 21ˢᵗ Century.* (Final Report. Washington DC, 2004), 11.

Chapter Seven:

War and Wisdom

This link between war and scientific knowledge is all but inseparable. Marine technologies developed for war often result in new discoveries in the civilian sector, and vice versa.

Forty years after she touched my social conscience, I still admire Rachel Carson's inter-tidal view of the marine environment and heed her warnings of environmental ignorance and carelessness. But the battle has moved from raising the alarm on the beaches of America to modeling and forecasting our impact upon planet Earth. I share Carson's passion for the sea, but I no longer share her view of it. She presented the field of oceanography to the public, but Rachel Carson had a marine biologist's view, as did Jacques Cousteau and almost every other person of their generation. They had the intuitive view. It is natural to view the sea from the perspective of the living organism.

Remote sensing and advances in oceanography changed my view. I now see the sea as a component of our surface domain, bounded by time and space, as determined by the forces of physics and geophysics. In my applied science view, the sea is akin to the Rubic's cube. There are so many inter-related variables to solve. Yet, the Rubic's cube is much simpler than the sea. This is why today's biological oceanographer is also skilled in mathematics and physics. This is why oceanography departments have meteorologists on faculty. This is why meteorologists and oceanographers monitor the environment over several orders of magnitude of time and space.

Despite these magnificent advancements in marine science, some oceanographers have lost a sense of passion. I share their sense of loss, but probably not for the same reasons. The heyday of mid-twentieth-century oceanography has passed, but this period was not my adult days, thus I do not feel their loss. For me, the problem is that considering the sea from the perspective of physics and geophysics does not stimulate my senses the way Rachel Carson, Jacques Cousteau, and other mass-media influences did. I have also lost my father, the foundation of my perception of the sea.

Some could argue the sense of loss is simple nostalgia, and that excitement returned to marine science when NASA made stunning breakthroughs in space-based ocean observing, but it is difficult to become passionate about sensors, even for an oceanographer like me. The engineers who design, build, and launch such technology may be passionate about these tools, but I'm not and neither is the general public. Besides, although NASA launched a view-changing ocean color satellite sensor in 1978, it did not launch another such sensor until almost twenty years later. For almost two decades, the field of sensing the sea's biology from space percolated along. Decades after they were first invented, the public has but cursory knowledge of them. These sensors demonstrated their value to scientists, but they have yet to capture the public's heart the way Jacques Cousteau did with technology in the 1950s and 60s.

Part of the problem may be that the United States now shares the vanguard of Earth observing with other nations. Even developing countries now have substantive spaceborne Earth-observing programs, with the result that they have become common. In the 1970s and 80s, America's commanding lead in Earth observing resulted in passionate public support. Today, the environmental space sector needs a Cousteau to reinvigorate it, much as early astronauts captivated us when they first orbited the planet and later landed on the moon. It was how they applied human flight technologies that inspired the public, not the technologies themselves. It is how we use

Earth-observing satellites that will inspire the masses, not the satellites themselves. The science community shunned Jacques Cousteau. Had he lived longer, and had he pursued perceived interests in observing the sea from space, today's Earth-observation programs could look significantly different. Cousteau had a knack for turning technology into wonder.

Then again, you could argue that excitement returned to the field of oceanography around the turn of the century. US administrators could argue this happened on 7 August 2000, when the US Congress signed the *Oceans Act of 2000* to establish a Commission on Ocean Policy, the first since the famed 1960s era Stratton Commission. Chaired by James D. Watkins, the US Commission on Ocean Policy submitted its final report, entitled *An Ocean Blueprint for the 21st Century*, to President Bush in September 2004. Five of the commission's sixteen directors held PhDs, as did its executive director, and this strong science representation showed in the commission's final report. The cover letter that accompanies the final report to the president reads like a page out of Rachel Carson. It includes warnings of environmental decline as a result of ineffective environmental management. It also recommends that the United States take an ecosystem-based approach to environmental management.

It took a few years for the report to resonate within Washington, but on 19 July 2010 President Obama announced the establishment of a national policy for stewardship of America's coastal and oceanic regions. His approach confirmed the science communities' re-gained traction within the senior halls of political power. As stated by John Holdren, director of the White House Office of Science and Technology Policy, "a national ocean policy reflects and affirms the invaluable role that science plays in the stewardship of these cherished resources."[50] The policy announcement included a commitment to strengthen the nation's ocean-observing systems. It also called for establishing a science-based ecosystem strategy. Almost sixty years after Rachel Carson recommended this approach, a US president implemented it.

The PhDs are back in the driver's seat, or as stated by Priscilla Brooks, of the Conservation Law Foundation: "For the first time in this country's history, we will have a national policy that aligns the great promise of our oceans with the great responsibility for managing them in a coordinated, thoughtful and sustainable fashion."[51]

The original 2004 Watkins Commission report demonstrates that a new breed of biological oceanographer has emerged in this twenty-first century. What may not be obvious by reading it is that the biologist now walks the hallways of war as the navy interweaves itself within the biological oceanographic community, just as it did with the marine physics community during World War II and the Cold War. Many of the directors of the latest US Commission on Ocean Policy hold PhDs, but the commission's Chair was a retired admiral of the US Navy. He was accompanied by a vice admiral who sat as a director. Although the Commission's 2004 final report echoes themes of Rachel Carson, the first of the seven objectives of the *Oceans Act of 2000* is "protection of life and property". Protection of the marine environment itself is third on the list, behind responsible stewardship of marine resources.

Seven months prior to President Obama announcing America's new ocean policy, the NATO Undersea Research Center in La Spezia, Italy, held a workshop for experts from 18 NATO countries, on coupling ocean optics, physics and biology in ecosystem

---

[50] R. Showstack, "Obama Administration Announces Ocean Policy," *EOS: Transactions of the American Geophysical Union*, 91, no. 31 (2010), 271.
[51] Ibid.

models. The color and transparency of the sea was front and center in the discussions. The environmental model they adopted for future research will be initialized by ocean color satellite data collected by the US Naval Research Laboratory's Hyperspectral Imager for the Coastal Ocean (HICO), the same sensor Japan quietly delivered to the International Space Station on behalf of the US government.[52]

Concurrently, researchers from the United States and China moved one step closer to determining water depth from ocean color, by devising a covert approach that does not require actual sampling of the targeted shore and beach zone.[53] Although their approach is based on advanced hyperspectral data, their unclassified report uses simpler multispectral data for demonstration purposes. History may be repeating itself. Just as the cutting edge of the civilian marine acoustics research community ducked behind the classified curtain of military funding over half a century ago, I suspect America's next cutting edge hyperspectral ocean color sensor will be classified, assuming it is not already.

This link between war and scientific knowledge is all but inseparable. Marine technologies developed for war often result in new discoveries in the civilian sector, and vice versa. The Special Branch that enlisted the services of James Bond author Ian Fleming in 1939, for example, had Britain's mandate for naval intelligence and meteorology. The field of ocean forecasting did not exist at that time, no one used the term *ocean intelligence,* and oceanography schools still focused on marine biology. Today, the same branch of the navy would likely be called METOC, in reference to meteorology and oceanography, and naval intelligence would be another entity to

---

[52] C.V.Trees et al., "Improving Optics–Physics–Biology Coupling in Ocean Ecosystem Models," *EOS: Transactions of the American Geophysical Union,* 91, no. 16 (2010), 144.
[53] Z.P. Lee et al, "Global Shallow-Water Bathymetry from Satellite Ocean Color Data," *EOS: Transactions of the American Geophysical Union,* 91, no 46 (2010), 429-430.

which METOC delivered intelligence about the present and future state of the maritime domain.

Regardless of what it is called, since the days of Ian Fleming, naval programs have produced or funded many inspiring technologies to view the sea. You may not be aware of them because it is the application of technology, not technology itself, that inspires us to the point of influencing our view. Unfortunately, as reflected in the character of my father and grandfather, the navy rarely talks about how it sees the sea. The public does not learn about such matters until decades after their development, when they become declassified and subsequently cross over into the civilian community. The pursuit of naval supremacy dictates this to be the case. Thus, components of our future view of the sea already exist within the classified world of ocean intelligence. There, they contribute to the security of billions while inspiring but a few.

Even within the civilian marine community, some argue that much of today's cutting-edge marine technology is still looking for a captivating application, the proverbial "killer app", to justify its existence. This helps to explain why the public has little knowledge of modern oceanographic technologies, even though oceanographic data and technologies are more accessible to the public today than they have ever been. During the Cold War, emerging technologies were applied to thwart a perceived nuclear attack and to some World War III. It is a matter of perspective. It is a matter of being driven by a captivating need so profound that its pursuit redefines an entire field of science. With certainty such need exists, and with equal certainty the sea remains a frontier of hidden knowledge. In 2002, Walter Munk, the physical oceanographer from Scripps, provided an example of such when discussing the subject of climate change: "The oceans are the principal reservoir for the storage of CO_2, of heat and of ignorance."[54] Nine years later the problem persists, as exemplified by the atmospheric scientist Galen McKinley: "One of the biggest challenges in asking how climate is affecting the ocean is simply a lack of data."[55] More than anything, this insufficient information issue, this ignorance, is what fuels the climate-change skeptics. We all know the climate is changing, but until we have the data required to quantify the inter-relationships of environmental cause and effect, we will disagree on the extent to which humans influence their environment.

In 2003, not long after the September 2001 terrorist attacks on the United States, the US Chief of Naval Operations was quoted as saying that the US Navy does not need a permission slip to fulfill its mission.[56] Sacrifices made then, and since, help justify such bold statements. Today's war against terrorism, however, is waged mostly on land and related naval missions are in littoral (i.e. coastal) waters, which are sovereign territory. If you are uncertain what this means, ask any Korean–North or South–or just ask any Canadian. In 1969, the US oil tanker *SS Manhattan* sailed through Canadian Arctic waters on behalf of an American oil company. The United States refused to officially request Canada's permission to enter the Northwest Passage. For Canada, this is a question of national sovereignty, and also of who owns untold natural resources in the region.

The Arctic sovereignty issue continues, with more recent events focusing on nuclear attack submarines travelling under

[54] Munk, "The Evolution of Physical Oceanography in the Last Hundred Years," 138.
[55] Galen McKinley, University of Wisconsin-Madison, personal communication. Also see G. McKinley et al., "Convergence of Atmospheric and North Atlantic Carbon Dioxide Trends On Multidecadal Timescales", *Nature Geoscience Letters,* DOI: 10.1038/NGEO1193 (2011).
[56] P. Renaud, "Oceanographic Information Superiority Through Battlespace Characterization," *Sea Technology* (December, 2003), 7.

Canadian Arctic waters, except this pertains to the submarines of several nations, not just the United States. International law states that you do indeed need a permission slip to sail the sovereign waters of a foreign nation. As a result, access may be denied. In the ocean intelligence sector, this leads to covert (i.e. secret) ocean monitoring techniques, such as spaceborne ocean-observing sensors, in order to acquire required environmental information. This need is not new. The Germans, for example, boldly established a weather station on the coast of Canada's Labrador in 1943, using a U-537 submarine. Canada did not discover its presence until the late 1970s.

Decades will pass before the civilian community gains accurate insight into the existing status of naval METOC operations. Does Canada, for example, actually need notification of intruding submarines or is it already detecting such vessels itself, via a network of monitored choke points (i.e. narrow passages) situated within the Canadian Arctic? If so, does Canada operate such stations alone or in concert with other nations? Who can say? Canada, the United States and other nations do not publicly define such installations. The public does, however, gain fragments of information, which may provide insight into advanced operational capabilities. On the other hand, such an approach can lead to conjecture and media hype, which influence public perception. Take, for example, an event that happened more than thirty years ago. Conjecture has resulted in it becoming oceanographic folklore. Previously, I discussed the launch of NASA's civilian Seasat satellite on 27 June 1978, which included the world's first spaceborne synthetic aperture radar sensor. What I did not note is that the satellite shut down on 10 October 1978, 106 days after its launch and only 70 days after it started to generate data.[57] A review board concluded the loss was a result of an electrical short in one of the satellite's slip ring assemblies.

---

[57] H.J. Kramer, *Observation of the Earth and its Environment: Survey of Missions and Sensors, 4th edition* (Berlin: Springer, 2002), 508.

To this day, the United States, which has the most technically advanced navy and one of the most advanced space programs on earth, has yet to launch another civilian spaceborne synthetic aperture radar sensor. Since the launch of Seasat more than thirty years ago, every other G7 country has followed in America's footsteps by launching at least one of them, either through its national space agency or through its regional agency. This covert sensor has proven to be profoundly practical. It detects military and civilian targets and features, penetrates clouds and operates at night. It can also detect small targets or survey synoptic-scale environmental processes. No other sensor/platform combination has all of its attributes.

The first of this non-American series was launched in 1991 by the European Space Agency, as a component of its ERS-1 Earth-observing satellite. It took them thirteen years to catch up to the US. Europe was followed shortly thereafter by Canada and Japan. Like Europe, these countries have since launched improved follow-on versions of their original sensors and certain European countries, notably Germany and Italy, now have their own national synthetic aperture radar programs. In 2009, the United States relaxed domestic licensing restrictions for such sensors. This acknowledged the disadvantage such restrictions placed on American companies and potentially allowed development of an American civilian spaceborne program. As of early 2011, however, such a program has yet to be announced.

Seasat was not the last Earth-observing satellite to live a short life. Several have lived even shorter lives, having died during the launch process, failed to attain their correct orbit, or switch on properly once in their prescribed orbit. But to put the brief life of Seasat in perspective, ocean-observing satellite sensors are designed to last three to seven years. Most do and often they continue to function years thereafter. NASA's Coastal Zone Color Scanner, for example, which also launched in 1978, continued to monitor the oceans until it ceased functioning in 1986. NASA's follow-on ocean color sensor, Seawifs, launched in 1997 through a contract awarded to a private company. A subsidiary continued to operate the satellite until NASA reported its demise on 15 February 2011, approximately fourteen years after its launch.

Since Seawifs, a multitude of national space agencies have launched satellite sensors designed to detect and quantify the color of the sea. As these sensors detect light in the visible component of the electromagnetic spectrum, they also detect other features visible to the naked eyes, such as surface waves appearing in sun glint. But like the human eye, such sensors cannot see through clouds and do not see at night. As a result, if your primary objective is to view surface waves, or surface manifestations of subsurface (i.e. internal) waves, such as those generated by nuclear attack submarines, then you'll want to deploy a synthetic aperture radar sensor. Preferably, one that has a fantastic view of all the seas, like one mounted on a satellite.

Imagine if you can, looking at a computer screen and seeing every deployed attack submarine on earth, regardless of nationality and location. Of course, you cannot accomplish this to operational standards with a single satellite. You need a constellation of radar sensors to do this, and that will cost you billions. This factor alone keeps most nations out of the game. A nation can diminish such expenditures by teaming with other nations that also have such sensors in space. Once gained, however, no nation is likely to share knowledge of how to detect and track submarines at sea for operational purposes. Even your closest allies are not that close.

Internal waves are generated routinely through natural processes, as well as by sub-surface features and objects, such as submarines. As a result, they are ubiquitous in the marine environment. Thus, in order to detect submarines with spaceborne radar sensors, in addition to having a multi-billion dollar budget, you need to acquire the means to differentiate natural from man-made waves. This means you require an in-depth knowledge of when, where, and why such waves are generated, naturally or otherwise.

This is why the US Office of Naval Research funds programs that produce atlases of internal waves and their properties.

In other words, in addition to understanding the hydrodynamics of submarines you need to know how an ocean works, at a very comprehensive level, and you require the means to forecast when and where internal waves occur naturally. To do so, you need not a regional but global ocean-observing system that routinely detects marine features at meso and smaller scales, twenty-four hours per day, seven days a week. As internal waves can be generated by forces associated with daily tides, such a system also requires a revisit time on the order of hours. I am not aware of any nation or group of nations that have such capability. If any should attain such stature, it will not alter my view that no nation rules the sea. Should they attain it well in advance of other superpowers, however, they could alter the balance of power that many believe stalemates the onset of World War III.

Part Two:

The Ocean We Perceive

Chapter Eight:

Navy Father, Civilian Son

My view of the sea was about to change, dramatically. If a change is as good as a vacation, as my father advised, then I was headed for the holiday from heaven.

Although a defining moment for both of us, we sat in silence as my father drove to the docks of Esquimalt harbor. I had spent all but four years of my life with him and was about to depart for another extended period of time. Yet, we stared at the pavement before us, speechless and seemingly without emotion. We could have parted company reminiscing about years spent together along the shores of the Atlantic and Pacific Ocean, but chin-wagging about the sea and experiences ashore was not something my father did. As a result, neither did I.

Esquimalt is a suburb of the City of Victoria. Its shore road borders the nation's west-coast naval fleet. As we approached the gates to Canadian Forces Base Esquimalt, my thoughts turned to times spent behind those gates as one of Esquimalt's countless navy brats. Although my father played a dominating role throughout those days, only two pieces of fatherly advice came to mind as we passed: "a change is as good as a vacation" and "don't join the navy."

My father rarely gave advice, and spoke few words when he did. Thus, although I was about to embark on a two month voyage on the Pacific Ocean, my first extended adventure on the high seas, I knew almost nothing about his lifetime at sea.

It was 1976, the year after the movie *Jaws* was released. With a newly minted bachelor of science degree in hand, I had landed my first post-university job as a galley steward on a coast guard ship headed for ocean weather station Papa. I was about to apply knowledge gained from four years of studying quantum mechanics and non-linear differential equations to serving meals, making beds, and living life at sea. Station Papa is simply a designated location in the Pacific Ocean, with no land in sight. From the perspective of a nautical chart it appears to be in the middle of nothing, almost a thousand miles from Victoria. Only those who sail the seas for a living will encounter it.

My father was not accustomed to chauffeuring, having recently retired from the Canadian Navy with two and a half rings. Lieutenant commander is a respectable rank, but not an outstanding achievement for a lifetime of naval service. When you consider his beginning, however, the magnitude of this accomplishment shines through. He started his career in a British naval academy at the age of eleven, only to end up in the Royal Navy as a lowly apprentice engine room artificer, near the bottom of the engineering pecking order. When he transferred from Britain's to Canada's navy in 1953, he jumped from petty officer to officer, but he spent World War II sweating in the hellishly hot and deafening engine rooms of His Majesty's warships.

He did not wear a lot of braid, but Lieutenant Commander Edward Whitehouse earned his rings the hard way—on cruisers, carriers, and frigates. Nick-named *Honest Ed* by his mates at sea, he never carried a briefcase, and he skipped the career-advancing networking stint at National Defence Headquarters in Ottawa, the nation's capital. As a lad, I remember him going to sea routinely, for months at a time, while my mother, five siblings and I lived life ashore. Although he did not grow a beard, he was the classic sailor imaged on a pack of Players Plain cigarettes, which he smoked throughout his time in the navy and years thereafter. Other than wearing a naval uniform, his physical appearance was unremarkable, although photos of his youth portray a man of moderate height perched on legs so skinny they could fit on a budgie bird. He filled out a bit in mid-life, but retained his short dark hair and claimed that he burst an ear drum while diving in his youth. This resulted in what we kids referred to as selective hearing, whereby he heard you when it suited him or he would reinterpret what you had said to him. It became a bit of a family joke as he twisted words and sentences while pleading with a smirk to have heard us incorrectly. As punishment for questioning his motives, he bequeathed me his legs, and my son his hearing ability.

Even after retiring, he could not break the life-long routine of watch duty. With my bedroom located on the bottom floor, I often awoke in the wee hours to the sound of him one deck above, standing watch at the kitchen table. Invariably, when I arose the next morning he had either left the house or was asleep in his bed. Telltale signs of his nocturnal activities included an ashtray of cigarette butts, an empty tea cup, and a table littered with a book or two and the day's newspaper, which had arrived at dawn.

He spent his post-naval days working for the local water utility, but said he wanted to be a writer. On weekends he strolled through second-hand book stores, carrying a leather bag for purchases he rarely made. At times he would leave home without it, preferring to stroll with his hands clasped behind his back in the classic naval at-ease position. It was the only retirement activity that consistently put a look of contentment on his face.

As a result of endless cups of tea and a genetic present from his British ancestors, my father's handwriting was shaky and almost illegible, just like mine. He bought an electric typewriter, but rarely used it. He typed a few pages, always on yellow paper, in conjunction with a writing course he took during retirement. But his teacher told him straight-up that he would never be a writer and that he was wasting both their time.

One morning while my mother watched in bewilderment, he placed the pages he had written in the living room fireplace and burned them. He refused to divulge their contents. By the time he died of heart failure, at the age of seventy two, he had yet to publish a word, and to the best of my knowledge there are no manuscripts lurking in the family attic. For whatever reason, Honest Ed chose not to share his knowledge and thoughts with this earthly world.

As the fourth son of a navy man, my view of the sea began as a child growing up in Halifax, Nova Scotia. Founded in 1749 by the British Admiralty, it remains a naval town to this day. In Halifax, I viewed the sea primarily from the docks of the city's yacht clubs and from the shores of its harbor.

Decades later I found myself driving towards the docks of Esquimalt, on the other side of the continent, with my father in the driver's seat. A steward ranks low on a ship's pecking order, but I didn't care. My view of the sea was about to change, dramatically. If a change is as good as a vacation, as my father advised, then I was headed for the holiday from heaven.

When the gates to Esquimalt's naval base passed, my father and I knew we would soon be at our destination. Esquimalt was his last posting in the navy, but he passed its gates without comment. Having raised me and paid for years of university, what was on his mind as he drove by? Was the hope that helped him survive the horrors of war a vision that one day he would raise a galley steward? He did not say. It was as if he was just running me over to the Canadian Forces Sailing Club for an afternoon sail on the Strait of Juan de Fuca, as he had done throughout my high school years.

He enrolled me in my first sailing class when I was twelve, but we only sailed together once, in the family's sailing dinghy. Although he had sailed the sea in almost every naval ship imaginable, he was uncomfortable in a fourteen-foot dinghy. I doubt his angst stemmed from the boat's cramped quarters. After all, he spent decades in the navy. It could have been due to the sailboat's constant heel in anything other than light winds, but more likely it was due to our proximity to the waterline and the bow's constant slicing of approaching waves as we beat out of the harbor to windward. To this day, I have no recollection of him swimming, diving, or simply wading in the surf. Put him *on* the water, but never *in* it.

When we reached the docks, a four hundred and fourteen foot long coast guard ship stood before us, and Canada's west coast naval fleet was in sight. As my father walked me to the ship's gangway, he showed no willingness to change his stoic way. We walked silently as I inhaled sea air and sensed my surroundings—tons of cold steel. Gulls flew overhead but the sounds of repair and replenishment dulled their cries.

We stopped at the foot of the gangway. For the second time in our lives, we stood together at the entrance to a massive ship. "Good luck", were the only words he spoke as he shook my hand. No advice, no reminiscing about similar experiences, no lectures on seamanship or words of encouragement and with certainty, no hug. Even the parting of a son could not release this battle-hardened Royal Navy sailor from the confines of naval discipline, almost a quarter century after he resigned from His Majesty's service.

As he shook my hand, I caught a slight glance and maybe a hint of a grin on his chalk-grey face. But it was his eyes that cause me to rethink this event throughout the decades since. In a faint display of emotion, he was trying to tell me something. His secrets of the sea remained safe, but in a span of time no longer than a puff of wind, the bonds of family emerged and held the air. For that moment, the docks went silent as generations of tradition engulfed us.

I like to think his expression was one of experience, but also one of pride. I had followed his advice and not joined the navy, but his fourth son had also followed him to sea, just as he had followed his father to sea, who in turn had followed his father—my great grandfather. He was losing a son but he was also fulfilling a family tradition. On the docks of Esquimalt harbor, some seven thousands miles from his British roots, my father repeated the act of generations before him. He passed the helm to a son. For a matter of seconds that day, we shared the tradition and a common view of the sea. He knew what I was about to experience and he knew that a life at sea is whatever you choose to make of it. It is not where you begin that defines you.

I had spent my youth sailing dinghies in harbors, but I boarded the ship feeling as inexperienced as a landlubber. Fortunately, you do not need to be a seasoned offshore sailor to develop respect for the sea and a sense of its incomprehensible power. You simply need to be caught in one severe storm. As a child I feared the unknown, but as a novice seaman riding out a storm on the Pacific Ocean I feared for the structural limits of the ship and the endurance and skills of its crew. In the officer's lounge of the coast guard ship, I sat in a corner as tethered tables and chairs broke loose and slid towards me like a wave running a beach. While spread eagle in my bunk at night, the only position that held me there, I heard the galley go to pieces and felt the ship shudder as it was struck by wave after wave. On one occasion, by morning, their unbridled power had twisted the ship's upper railings.

Riding out your first storm at sea is surreal. It unnerves you and causes you to fear for your life. But it also invigorates. It is an adrenaline-fueled adventure, and like all extreme adventures, it feels like you are taking a walk to the edge of life. One of my sisters-in-law, who is prone to sea sickness, once stated that the reason why people like to sail is that it feels so good when you disembark. Regardless of whether you get seasick, there is truth to this. Returning from an adventure at sea reminds you of how great life can be, and eventually, unless you are prone to seasickness, it instills a passion to return.

I survived the weather ship cruise as a galley steward and launched my career upon it. During the idle hours of keeping an ocean weather station, I became friends with the ship's chief and only oceanographer. He worked for a company that filled the position on a contract basis and the company was desperately short of contractors.

Although I had majored in chemistry and mathematics, I had also graduated from the University of British Columbia, which started the nation's first oceanography department. At the time, I thought it strange that someone with no formal training in oceanography would be offered such a position. It did not take me long, however, to discover the inter-relationship between oceanography, chemistry, mathematics, physics, and the navy.

I quit my steward's job after the first cruise, and after two weeks of intensive shore-based training, I shipped out on the next weather ship as its oceanographer. I had an en suite cabin to myself, which a steward serviced while I performed my oceanographic duties. At mealtime, I sat at the captain's table. Every person needs at least one major break in their career, and this was mine. As my father learned before me, life is not linear. It comprises a handful of defining moments punctuated by the rest of your life. The gangway to weather station Papa was a defining moment in my life, and my father was there to witness it. He steered me away from the navy and spared me the life he endured, but he also showed me the sea. With a schedule of approximately two months at sea followed by one ashore, over a two-year period I sailed aboard the Canadian Coast Guard weather ships CCGS *Vancouver* and *Quadra*. With swaying decks, shrinking shoreline and the obligatory fire drill, the beginning of every cruise was a time of transition. My land-based environment shrank from view and was replaced by another. During this stage, I appreciated the fact that in addition to acquiring my father's love of the sea, I also inherited his sea legs. It is difficult to enjoy the sea, or even function, when you cannot eat or walk without vomiting. Weather station Papa was a change of life, but not a vacation in the classic sense. Conditions often involved "a heavy swell or sea, low visibility, and a general lack of sunshine."[58]

---

[58] J. Proc, *Radio Communications and Signal Intelligence in the Canadian Navy—Weather Ships* (http://jproc.ca/rrp/index.html), 14.

My total time on the water now equates to years, but I have only been sea sick once, and it was not aboard the weather ships. It happened the day after I pulled a late evening anchor watch with a fellow sailor. We drank rum and watched the stars on the foredeck while holed-up in Rogue's Roost—one of the Atlantic's most memorable maritime hideaways. Finding and getting into Rogue's Roost is difficult without running aground, but once you're in, you are snug for the night. This night, we were aboard my brother's forty-two foot wooden schooner *Hakada*. We kept my brother-the-captain awake that night, and as punishment I sense he deliberately set to heavy seas early next morning, making the voyage back to Halifax via the ever-rolling inner passage. I have never been hung over on one of my brother's boats since, at least not while he was aboard.

After the first day or two at sea aboard the weather ships, I was at ease with my daily routine, showing up for duty, running the oceanographic sampling program, playing monopoly in the officer's mess at night, and riding out whatever weather we experienced.

My inaugurating cruise as a galley steward had ended up working to my favor. It allowed me to interact with the crew in a manner you cannot do as an officer, and I discovered that the average deck hand is tough, but not as rough as he looks and sounds. Initially, my thoughts focused on *newly-minted college boy gets the crap beaten out of him*. Thus, my strategy was to keep a low profile and not make too much eye contact. The crew, however, initiated introductions by asking about my place of birth, not my education. It seemed as if half of them were from the east coast. I had never met any of them before, but we had a common bond as Atlantic Canadians. In the crew's lounge at night even the Newfoundlanders seemed like distant relatives. Then again, you need to be a right-some miserable bugger to alienate a Newfoundlander in a bar. There is a saying that the further east you travel in Canada the friendlier the people get. I concur.

Unlike the occasional alcoholic crewman who drank himself blind when ashore and suffered for it at sea, I took well to the lifestyle. I suppose my father's silent guidance had something to do with it, having run his household as if it were a ship–with himself as its captain and my mother his first mate. But I also took advice from fellow officers. During a drunken evening of mad monopoly in the officer's lounge, for example, I was advised that at weather station Papa you either become alcoholic, or gay, or you take up fishing.

By the third cruise, I was bringing home over twenty-five pounds of Pacific salmon per trip–freshly filleted on the fantail, and smoked in the ship's unoccupied helicopter hangar. I did not fish before weather station Papa and I have not fished since, but I still savour the taste of freshly smoked Pacific salmon.

My foremost problem as Papa's resident oceanographer was trying to prevent the officers and crew from taking the plastic bags that protected my bathythermograph sensors. Once launched overboard, this expendable sensor measures water temperature as it free-falls through the water column. The sensor's protective storage bag was the perfect freezer bag for the crew's catch of the day, so I kept an eye on them!

The matter seems trivial, but without the bag the exposed sensor may degrade in sea air, and water temperature data are critical to oceanographic sampling programs. They are used to determine water density, which in turn provides insight into the structure and dynamics of water masses. Water temperature is also the most important oceanographic parameter in antisubmarine warfare operations as it affects how sound travels through water and therefore affects the performance of acoustic sensors. Such sensors are used routinely to operate allied submarines and also to find those belonging to the enemy, which was the Soviet Union during my weather ship days.

Certain crew-related issues could be dealt with easily, such as the rare occasion when the winch man showed up for his watch so drunk that he hung onto the winch handle to stay upright. But the plastic bag issue arose routinely, and it involved a significant number of officers and crew. It had to be approached with measured response. I got along with the crew, but regardless of your rank or birth you don't want to piss them off *en masse*. They had their means of hanging any officer out to dry. In my case, it involved my bucket of bottle-cast messengers.

My foremost responsibility as the ship's oceanographer was dropping a wire to just above the bottom of the Pacific Ocean, 4,220 meters below the ship's keel. As the winch man let out the wire, I attached water sampling bottles to it at specified locations. Each bottle had a brass weight attached to it, called a messenger, which when released dropped down the wire until it hit the sample bottle below it. This caused the bottle to close and thereby collect a sample of water at that depth, but it also released that bottle's messenger.

I started the chain reaction by dropping the first messenger down the wire by hand from the ship's oceanographic platform, several decks above sea level. On it went, bottle after bottle, messenger after messenger, until the messenger attached to the second last bottle triggered the bottom bottle. The wire was so long that I could drop the first messenger and go for lunch, returning just before the bottom bottle closed.

Much of the ship participated in the day's bottle cast, from engineer to boatswain, from helmsman to officer of the watch and executive officer. It could be a difficult maneuver for a large ship at sea. If the wire drifted too much under the keel, when the winch man hauled it up the bottles would catch on the keel or scrape along the hull, which caused them to detach from the wire and sink to Davy Jones' locker, at significant financial cost. The bottles themselves were not expensive, but the precision thermometers attached to them were. On days when we started a cast in suitable seas but finished in strong winds, I could lose thousands of dollars of equipment if the officer on watch could not hold position.

Even the captain kept an eye on the bottle cast, except on the days I had ticked off the crew, and therefore could not find my bucket of messengers. There were no bottle casts on those days. The bucket mysteriously disappeared, and no member of the crew had a clue where it went. Depending upon what it was that had them in a funk, it could take a day or two to reappear. This never occurred while at station Papa itself, but on occasion the bucket disappeared on the trip home, after we had been at sea for almost two months. This prevented me from doing bottle casts along the homeward route, which got us to port that much sooner.

On the first day home from a cruise, I felt like I was still at sea, with a sense of ground swaying beneath me. For the first few hours I compensated by not driving a vehicle, choosing instead to ask my father to fetch me from the docks. Each ride home was almost as silent as our first ride to the docks, but our relationship had changed. The life I had with my father for almost a quarter century came to an end when I became gainfully employed. A steady income provided the means to move out of my parent's house. The aging man who sailed the seas for half a century stayed ashore, while his now independent son went to sea. On occasion during my leave, however, my father and I sat together at his beloved kitchen table, always with a cup of tea in hand, as I told of my adventures and experiences as an oceanographic technician.

By recalling my adventures, I began to appreciate what my father would have known the first day we parted company at the gangway to a weather ship, but chose not to tell. Something my grandfather and great grandfather likely knew. Something all sailors know. Being attracted to the sea is not about choosing a career. At sea there is only you and your ship, the sky above and the seemingly bottomless sea, for as far as the eye can see. Being attracted to the sea is about escaping the mundane of daily ritual and being in tune with planet Earth. For me, the sense is similar to walking through the forests of British Columbia, except at sea the loss of land to stand on generates a sense of adventure that is unparalleled on land. In both cases, however, the absence of urban distractions focuses your senses on the environment that engulfs you.

My father would sit at the kitchen table and listen to my stories, smoking his Players and drinking his tea. At times he rewarded me with a nod or smile, while veiled in puffs of smoke against a background of nicotine-stained wallpaper. Otherwise, he simply sat and listened. My adventures undoubtedly touched upon aspects of the shipboard life he experienced for decades, but chose not to discuss. He provided no stories of similar experiences, no questions of whether I saw this or that, no advice on how to improve my seamanship, and nothing to share a laugh about. Unlike most people who ask me about life as an oceanographer, he never asked if I scuba dive. His view of the sea did not involve frolicking with dolphins, and years before I realized it myself, he knew that neither would mine.

In hindsight, my experiences at Papa probably had similarities to what he experienced during his first few weeks at sea, when he was just sixteen years old. Thereafter, his naval experiences were nothing to chuckle about over a cup of tea. By the time he was my twenty-three years, he had already sailed on HMS *Raleigh*, *Victory* and *Hawkins*. He had also survived war at sea. His experiences were something he was trying to bury, not reminisce about.

Grandfather William Whitehouse was the son of an English seaman. He became a stoker in the Royal Navy, and according to my father's youngest sister, like my father, my grandfather was a man of few words. Apparently, in the Royal Navy you learn not to speak your mind. Like my great grandfather, Grandfather Whitehouse went by his middle name–George, which he gave to my father as his middle name, who in turn gave it to me as mine.

My father went by his first name–Edward–and he never addressed me as George. On 5 July 1933, when Edward was barely eleven years old, George removed his son from the family home and shipped him off to The Royal Hospital School. The facility continues today as it was then, a boarding academy located in Holbrook, Ipswich. Edward never lived with his mother again. She died six years later, during child birth, when she was thirty-eight years old. Nor did he see his siblings again, until years later when they were no longer children. His sisters were not told he had been sent to an academy, or that he was not permitted to return home.

The Holbrook facility was established as a school for the children of Royal Navy seamen and it was run with military precision. In the early 1930s most of Holbrook's students were orphans who were accepted with the understanding that upon graduation they would join the Royal Navy. Each student was assigned a number, a locker, a nautical uniform, and a cot in a fifty-bed dormitory. The daily routine, which began at 06:45 and ended at 20:15, was "very strict but fair".[59]

Edward was discharged from the Holbrook facility on 31 December 1937. Three days later he joined the Royal Navy, stationed at His Majesty's barracks at Chatham. George advised him to sign on for engine room duty as it paid an extra shilling a day. During the years that followed, Edward bitterly regretted having taken this advice.

He was assigned to the Mechanical Trainer Establishment and the HMS *Pembroke* depot. Edward's mother died during his time there. The Royal Navy gave him twenty-four hours leave to attend her funeral, but his two sisters were not permitted even this basic moment of closure. Within months of his mother's death, Edward was fighting World War II at sea, but before the war there was a need to keep the men occupied. In part, this was accomplished through drill tasks. When assigned the task of cleaning the parade square, for example,

---

[59] P. Bevand, "Jim Taylor: Wartime Service in H.M.S *Hood*," *BBC News*, January 4, 2006.

men had to march forward and backward, and pick up every cigarette butt they could find. As smoking was strictly forbidden at Holbrook, Chatham is likely where Edward acquired his habit of smoking two packs of Players Plain cigarettes per day.

When Edward returned from China on HMS *London*, in 1949, he was assigned various shore stations, the last being a naval school in Scotland. Twenty years after George placed him in a British naval academy, he was back in one. For two years he endured the childhood memories this must have triggered, then he resigned from the Royal Navy. His employer had given him a vacation from the sea, but after sixteen years under the influence of the Royal Navy, Edward realized it was time for a change.

As an ordinary seaman in the Royal Navy, George had likely suffered the same lifestyle as Edward. When George's wife died at a young age, he was unable to cope as a single parent while working at sea. He was forced to take the unthinkable and for many the unbearable step of dissolving his remaining family by dispersing his two daughters and other two sons to other homes. Edward's sister Edna, for example, was shipped off to Portsmouth and Vera to London, to homes of people they did not know. Eventually, George married his housekeeper and reunited his children into a new family. Edward was not included, though, because by that time he was at sea with the Royal Navy. Edward believed George remarried to silence neighborhood gossip about his relationship with his housekeeper. But on his deathbed, George abandoned his tight-lipped manner and harsh outer layer. During his final moments on earth he confided in his daughters, and told them that he only remarried to keep his children from being placed in a public home. Edward's account reflects bitterness, George's paternal love.

One of Edward's final acts on British soil, just prior to boarding a Southampton-based liner headed for the port of Montreal, was to pay George a visit. What the two tight-lipped and battle-hardened navy men spoke of is known only by them; both of whom are long gone. My mother concluded the two parted on good terms, but until the day he died my father never spoke to me about my grandfather. Not a word. Nor did he speak about the mechanics of life at sea with the Royal Navy. He told me nothing about the ships, their equipment and the techniques the navy used to gain strategic and tactical advantage. Being in the engine room, and of the enlisted class, he had little knowledge of naval tactics and ocean intelligence.

Although he did not share his maritime knowledge, my father gave me perceptions of the sea. I acquired them before I went to weather station Papa, before I studied oceanography in graduate school, and before I specialized in viewing the sea from spaceborne satellites. My father did not see the sea as such, nor did Jacques Cousteau, Rachel Carson, Ian Fleming, or a slew of other mid-twentieth century celebrities. Unlike my science-based spaceborne view and my father's classified naval view, however, these celebrities collectively generated the public's de facto twentieth century view of the sea. But regardless of public profile, we have a common bond–a defining story of the sea that arose as a result of being in the right place at the right time. We all have perceptions of the sea, but some stand taller than others.

Chapter Nine:

The Green Pioneer

Rachel Carson was green decades before anyone recognized the word as anything other than a color. And although she may not be a household name among our youth, they unknowingly witness the everlasting benefits of her work.

Frederick Hunt's hypothesis of a subject percolating along until it is ripe for major advancement also applies to the field of oceanography, as does his point that major breakthroughs occur over a relatively short period of time. For oceanography, this period was World War II and the onset of the Cold War that followed.

In 1951, the science writer Rachel Carson became the first person in the west to present the subject of oceanography to the public in a manner that changed not only perception of the sea, but also public understanding of ecosystems and the dynamics of the sea. Whether it was a conscious act or not, from the eastern shores of the United States, Rachel Carson captured the imagination with her passion for the environment. Scientists often write factually about the sea in their peer-reviewed journals, and others have stimulated our imagination with poetic accounts of their marine experiences, but Rachel Carson accomplished both. This is a rare feat.

Prior to 1951, Rachel Carson was an unknown biologist. She was also a talented science writer, in the right place at the right time. Carson synthesized knowledge emerging from America's renowned oceanographic institutions and rode the field's growth curve all the way to the early 1970s. As summarized by Carson in 1961:

"The awakening of active interest in the exploration of the sea came during the Second World War, when it became clear that our knowledge of the ocean was dangerously inadequate. We had only the most rudimentary notions of the geography of the undersea world over which our ships sailed and through which submarines moved. We knew even less about the dynamics of the sea—These vastly accelerated studies soon began to show that many of the old conceptions of the sea were faulty, and by the mid-point of the century a new picture had begun to emerge."[60]

Rachel Carson did not skin dive, scuba dive, sail the seas, or even go to sea. She once participated in a ten day research cruise to Georges Bank, which is off the coast of Massachusetts. She also dove underwater once, using a diving helmet, not scuba gear, while hanging onto a boat ladder. Otherwise, her sea experience was limited to shore-based views of the Atlantic seaboard of the United States. She was an indifferent swimmer and not fond of boats.[61] Yet, she inspired us to view the sea as a network of ecosystems, rather than as a source of food and means of transportation and war. She also showed us the link between marine biology and oceanography, using her now famous poetic style:

"There is nothing static about an ecosystem; something is always happening. Energy and materials are being received, transformed and given off. The living community maintains itself in a dynamic rather than static balance."[62]

Although this approach to marine environmental management is now common, Carson was on the vanguard, and she positioned her view to present a unique perspective. She recognized this as early as

---

[60] L. Lear, ed., Lost *Woods: The Discovered Writing of Rachel Carson* (Boston: Beacon Press, 1998), 102.

[61] L. Lear, *Rachel Carson: Witness for Nature* (New York: Henry Holt, 1997), 263.

[62] Lear, ed., *Lost Woods: The Discovered Writing of Rachel Carson*, 231.

1942, more than a decade before North America saw the likes of Jacques Cousteau:
"I believe that most popular books about the ocean are written from the viewpoint of a human observer–usually a deep-sea diver or sometimes a fisherman–and record his impressions and interpretations of what he saw. I was determined to avoid this human bias as much as possible."[63]

As a child growing up in Pennsylvania, Rachel Carson had a strong affinity towards nature and wanted to be a writer. Her first publication came at the age of eleven, when she wrote about the bravery and death of a Canadian flying instructor during World War I. The story was published in a children's magazine and was based on a letter her brother wrote while serving overseas. Her first literary sale happened while barely a teenager, in 1921, but she did not earn enough to make a living from freelance writing until the early 1950s, about a decade before she died.

As an undergraduate, Carson majored in biology at the Pennsylvania College for Women (now Chatham University) and went on to graduate school at Johns Hopkins, Maryland, where in 1932 she received a master's degree in zoology.

In addition to Massachusetts, throughout her career Carson spent time at coastal areas of North Carolina, Florida, and Maine. As an adult she lived in Silver Spring, Maryland, but starting in the early 1950s, she spent her summers at her beloved seaside cottage at Southport Island, Maine, which is where she obtained material for and wrote much of her third book on the sea. It is also where she first discovered, and subsequently developed, her passion for preservation of the terrestrial environment.

Although Carson was trained in science, she did not work as a research scientist. After graduating from Johns Hopkins, she worked for what subsequently became the US Fish and Wildlife Service.

---

[63] Ibid., 55.

Even as an undergraduate Carson was recognized for her ability to present technical subjects to the layperson. This contributed to her subsequent rise within the ranks of the civil service and to her novel view of the sea.

It was not long after graduate school that Carson established herself as a freelance marine author, with *Under the Sea Wind* in 1941 and then *The Sea Around Us* in 1951. Her third and final marine book, *The Edge of the Sea,* appeared in 1955, seven years before the release of her epic book–*Silent Spring.*

Released during World War II, only 2,000 copies of *Under the Sea Wind* sold before it went out of print in 1946. But her next book, *The Sea Around Us,* was a stunning success, with the magazine *The New Yorker* paying more than Carson's annual government salary to serialize nine of the book's chapters, prior to publication of the book itself. This exposure provided important public recognition, perhaps crucial.[64]

Carson became an award-winning literary star in the United States as a result of this introduction to the field of oceanography. The year following its release, she and her agent seized the opportunity to re-release the poorly selling *Under the Sea Wind.* Forty thousand copies sold before it was re-published. And by the time sections of *Under the Sea Wind* were reproduced in the 14 April 1952 edition of *Life* magazine, *The Sea Around Us* was enjoying its thirty-first consecutive week as America's leading non-fiction best seller.

Her third and final marine book, *The Edge of the Sea,* was also a commercial success, but among the three *The Sea Around Us* remains the most prominent. By the time *The Edge of the Sea* came out in 1955, *The Sea Around Us* had sold about one million copies in the United States alone. No one having a marine science focus has

---

[64] Linda Lear, author of *Rachel Carson: Witness for Nature*, personal communication.

come close to this feat in the more than half century since, and no one is likely to.

Although Carson wrote three books pertaining to the sea, only *The Sea Around Us* focuses on the subject of oceanography. It presents the physical, chemical, biological, and geological dynamics of the sea, not from a perspective of the human eye, like Jacques Cousteau's films, but from the perspectives of time and space. Her other two marine books are largely about marine biology.

The Sea Around Us is the only Carson marine book I recall reading in my youth. I cannot recall whether my older brother purchased a copy of the book or borrowed it from a library, and neither can he. But with certainty it was he and not my father who brought it into our household. Although my father spent his life at sea, I do not recall him reading about it when at home. Perhaps when ashore, his frame of mind was similar to that of fishermen who live in the Newfoundland village I once inhabited. Although their homes are situated on waterfront property, they build them with the large windows facing the street, not the water.

I make the distinction between marine biology and oceanography because it was *The Sea Around Us* that established Carson as an acclaimed author. Of course no one thinks of Rachel Carson as an oceanographer, including Carson herself, but she became a literary great when she viewed the sea from an oceanographic perspective. Carson realized the difference: "I'm primarily a marine biologist, not an oceanographer. With oceanography you come up against physics, mineralogy, geology and a lot of other 'ologies. I know something of them, but biology is my main field."[65]

This quotation provides additional insight into the magnitude of Carson's accomplishment. Just bringing one aspect of science to

---

[65] C. Durgin, "Overnight Miss Carson Has Become Famous," *Boston Daily Globe,* July 20, 1951, 4.

public attention is a major accomplishment, but a multitude of aspects, simultaneously, is monumental. As alluded to by Carson: "As the frontiers of science expand, there is inevitably an increasing trend toward specialization, in which all the mental faculties of a man or group of men are brought to bear upon a single aspect of some problem. But there is fortunately a counter tendency, which brings different specialists together to work in cooperation. Oceanographic expeditions commonly include biologists, chemists, physicists, geologists, and meteorologists, so diverse are the problems presented by one aspect of the earth's surface."[66]

Rachel Carson introduced us to the dynamics of the sea in 1951; yet, almost half a century thereafter, perception, not fact or understanding of what drives the environment, continued to dominate the popular view. She synthesized volumes of scientific information into a poetic description of oceanography, but by the mid-to-late 1970s, during oceanographic cruises on the Pacific Ocean I observed a lack of such knowledge among the ship's crew. My father's generation and the baby boomers that followed continued the tradition, growing up uncertain of even how many oceans there are.

In defense of my father's generation, when Carson's book was released, few could know that she was describing the genesis of a new field of applied science—one that we would subsequently perceive as fundamental to the security and preservation of the planet. Besides, in my father's case, he and his fellow British shipmates were preoccupied at the time, having just escaped death in the soon-to-be communist China. And then came the Russians. Throughout the 1950s and early 60s, real and perceived threats of the expanding Soviet Bear drove great advances in oceanography. However, much of it occurred within the classified world of naval intelligence. The public was largely oblivious to emerging oceanographic frontiers of relevance to naval warfare. Carson was aware of some of it though. In

---

[66] Lear, ed., *Lost Woods: The Discovered Writing of Rachel Carson*, 166.

1951, while noting that the US Navy conducted a great deal of top secret ocean research during World War II, she said: "We learned more about the sea in those few years than we had for a long time previously."[67]

Oceanographic knowledge continued to expand throughout the Cold War. During its height, my then Canadian navy father experienced the benefits and treachery of oceanographic knowledge in the hands of superpowers, while his baby-boomer children grew up oblivious to both. By then, public interest in the ocean was gravitating toward the likes of the color television and the adventures of Jacques Cousteau.

But there is another reason why Rachel Carson is not widely recognized today for her captivating book on oceanography. Shortly after she published *The Sea Around Us,* Carson again proved her ability to be in the right place at the right time. She again proved my father's belief that a change is as good as a vacation. Rachel Carson once more demonstrated her talent as a poetic science writer, and she did it in absolutely massive proportion. But not within the marine world per se.

The musician Bryan Adams sings the glories of the *Summer of '69,* but the '60s summer that stands out in my mind is 1962, the year Rachel Carson demonstrated we are unwittingly poisoning the planet we inhabit. After publication of *The Sea Around Us,* Rachel Carson changed her focus from sea to land. Through study of scientific papers and public reports, she concluded that indiscriminate use of herbicides and insecticides was killing not only the intended targets but also other components of terrestrial and aquatic environments. She published her findings in a book entitled *Silent Spring,* and she blamed the problem on chemical companies, the politicians they supported, and bungling bureaucrats. And instead of using synthetic chemicals to deal with biological pests, she advocated

---

[67] Durgin, "Overnight Miss Carson Has Become Famous," 4.

natural means to control them and gave examples where such biological approaches were successful.

Essentially, Carson showed the public that Earth's water, land, air, and human inhabitants are components of a single entity, and she did so in a manner that disturbs me to this day. I sense this was her objective–to cause us to think about consequences of our actions. But I doubt she imagined her book would eventually receive recognition as the start of North America's environmental movement.

Just prior to publication as a book, most of *Silent Spring* was serialized in three successive editions of *The New Yorker* magazine. By Christmas of 1962, the book was selling at a rate of more than 100,000 copies per week. It became a phenomenon and Carson a celebrity. In 1963, she appeared on *CBS Reports*, to an audience of ten to fifteen million people.[68] She also appeared before a special U.S. Senate Committee on the use of pesticides in the environment.

Rachel Carson died of breast cancer eighteen months after publishing her warning against indiscriminate use of carcinogenic or otherwise toxic pesticides. Although more than one million copies of *Silent Spring* sold by the time she died, Carson did not live long enough to reap the glory this book would have bestowed upon a longer career. She did not live long enough to once again study and write about her beloved marine environment.

Carson's heart belonged to the sea. As she put it, "I guess birds come next to my heart after fish, and then cats and dogs".[69] In 1948, she stated that her "consuming interest happens to be the ocean and its life" and she once described herself "as a marine biologist whose actual profession is writing rather than biology".[70]

As was the case for *Silent Spring*, Rachel Carson collected the material for her marine-related books by studying and

---

[68] Lear, *Rachel Carson: Witness for Nature*, 450.
[69] Durgin, "Overnight Miss Carson Has Become Famous," 4.
[70] Lear, *Rachel Carson: Witness for Nature,* 154.

synthesizing scientific papers and public reports from her office, home, and the libraries of New England and Washington D.C. She also corresponded with some of the most renowned experts of her time. From this perspective, she is somewhat of an enigma as she curiously developed a passion for the sea from shore, and she did it at a time when it was difficult for a woman to be taken seriously in her chosen profession.

Obtaining a graduate science degree and related employment in the mid-twentieth century was uncommon for a female. In his 1951, front-page review of *The Sea Around Us*, for example, *Boston Daily Globe* writer Cyrus Durgin pens two brief paragraphs about the book before turning his well-meaning attention to the fact that Carson is female and an unmarried one at that. The culture Carson experienced at the time is reflected in his fourth paragraph:

"Would you imagine a woman who has written about the seven seas and their wonders to be a hearty, physical type? Not Miss Carson. She is small and slender, with chestnut hair and eyes whose color has something of both the green and the blue of sea water. She is trim and feminine, wears a soft pink nail polish and uses lipstick and powder expertly, but sparingly."[71]

Durgin's article appears on the front page, next to that day's headline: *"U.S. Rejects Red Demand That Troops Quit Korea"*. The headline occupies three quarters of the front page's top banner. Carson's photo occupies the remainder.

I imagine Carson's life having similarities to that of women portrayed in the movie *Mona Lisa Smile*, which is set in an American all-girls college in the 1950s. Carson put it this way:

"People often seem to be surprised that a woman should have written a book about the sea. This is especially true, I find, of men. Perhaps they have been accustomed to thinking of the more exciting fields of scientific knowledge as exclusively masculine domains. In fact, one

---

[71] Durgin, "Overnight Miss Carson Has Become Famous," 4.

of my correspondents not long ago addressed me as 'Dear Sir'– explaining that although he knew perfectly well that I was a woman, he simply could not bring himself to acknowledge the fact."[72]

Prior to her death, Carson continued to be recognized throughout the United States for her expertise in marine science. After all, one does not become a marine science reviewer for *The New York Times* without such recognition. Yet, *Silent Spring* dwarfs her marine reputation. Even the cover of a comprehensive biography refers to Carson as the author of *Silent Spring*.

Herbicides and insecticides are not used in the sea, and although they may enter coastal waters in rivers, streams, and groundwater, intuitively people do not link Rachel Carson's two renowned publications. I do, but even in my case, it was not until graduate school that I applied *Silent Spring* to the dynamics of the sea.

Baby boomers grew up with DDT and PCBs. The latter are not referenced in Carson's work, but like DDT are chlorinated hydrocarbons. They are also known for their potentially lethal toxicity. Most adults do not know the chemical nomenclature for DDT or PCB, but as a result of *Silent Spring* most know DDT is synonymous with inadvertent death in our forests, streams and lakes.[73]

I cannot say how many people realize that Rachel Carson first brought the potentially lethal nature of the chlorinated hydrocarbon to public consciousness. But I can say that her work disturbed me to such an extent that I devoted five years of my life to an investigation of the behavior of carcinogenic hydrocarbons in the aquatic environment. The 1983 final report for this work was accepted as my doctoral thesis in oceanography. The external examiner came from

---

[72] Lear, ed., *Lost Woods: The Discovered Writing of Rachel Carson*, 77.

[73] DDT is an abbreviation for dichlorodiphenyltrichlorethane. PCB stands for polychlorinated biphenyl.

Woods Hole Oceanographic Institution, which is where Rachel Carson studied marine biology.

My graduate research took place on the east coast, along the shores and coastal waters of the Atlantic Ocean. This happened immediately after my time sailing the coastal waters of British Columbia as an oceanographic technician. It caused me to move more than four thousand kilometers from the docks of Esquimalt and my parent's home. A graduate student has money for beer, shelter, and food, but not for trips across the continent. My days of sharing maritime adventures with my father, at the family's kitchen table, came to an end.

I doubt either of my parents understood the concept of graduate school and the research it entailed. At times, we would talk by phone as my mother asked me to explain again how a full-time student earns money to live on, and what job I hoped to turn my research into. They were, however, genuinely proud and excited the day I was bestowed the title of doctor. I recall few events that caused my father to show emotion, but this was one. On that day, even my west-coast brother tipped his hat, with a cross-continent shipment of a case of my favorite west-coast beer, encased in countless feminine napkins for protection. An odd choice for packing material, but not for *Chico*, who lived his teenaged-years in the fast lane. I was the fourth son, but felt like the older brother on dark early mornings, when I was awoken by a rap on the ground-floor bedroom window we shared in high school. After I unlocked the window, he would crawl in over the desk I used for studying, feeling no pain and grinning.

Chico didn't read books like *The Sea Around Us* and *Silent Spring*, but unbeknownst to him, and countless others, Rachel Carson continues to influence his life. Read *Silent Spring* now and sense its presence as you go about your daily routine. Witness evidence of the book in what you read, listen to, and experience. Like Jacques

Cousteau, Rachel Carson influenced how we view the sea, but unlike Cousteau, she also influenced how we live our lives.

As my son and I walked together through the changing room of our local gym one day in 2009, he appeared oblivious to the fact that the song he was listening to over the gym's sound system was one of the remakes of the 1970 Joni Mitchell classic *Big Yellow Taxi*. Two lines of the song, "Hey farmer farmer, Put away that DDT now", are likely a reflection of Carson's influence upon Mitchell, given that the original lyrics were written within the time frame of *Silent Spring*'s media profile. How many millions of people have been touched by Carson's cause as a result of Mitchell's heart-felt promotion? And who can say how or whether this contributed to the decision to ban DDT in the United States, which happened two years after the song was first released? Unlike Jacques Cousteau, Rachel Carson did not have her own television series, but the environmental movement of the 1970s and beyond spread her view on her behalf.

The United States stopped manufacturing DDT in 1972, and in 2004 the international Treaty on Persistent Organic Pollutants resulted in a global ban, even though it was used to great success during World War II, to control disease-carrying lice and mosquitoes. In 1948, Paul Mueller received the Nobel Prize for his 1930's discovery of its value as a pesticide.

To this day, even though many species of malaria-carrying mosquitoes have developed a resistance to DDT, it is still recognized as an effective means to combat this disease. In 2006, this led the World Health Organization to reverse its thirty-year-old policy on the pesticide by endorsing its proper use indoors. Rachel Carson did not advocate banning pesticides. She advocated proper use and only when necessary.

PCB production was also banned in the 1970s. Again, this family of chemicals is not associated with Carson's book, but indirectly her warnings played a role in raising the alarm regarding their potential environmental impact.

A few months after my son and I went to the gym together, I was having my hair cut by a twenty-something stylist while my teenage daughter stood by. I asked whether either had heard of Rachel Carson. Neither of them had. Given their age, their response was understandable, but while staring in the mirror before me, I realized they did not need to recognize her name in order to reap the benefits of her work. There and then, I lost all doubt as to whether Rachel Carson remains among us today.

While listening to my daughter tell the stylist how much she liked her new hair color, I was staring at the April 2009 issue of *Veranda* magazine, which lay before me on the stylist's mirrored cabinet. It featured an article on Rachel Carson and presented her as an environmental visionary and champion.[74] The company eBay took out the article's accompanying advertising space with a full page ad in which the title "30 Days of green" occupied two thirds of the space, in various shades of green. *Veranda* itself also chose to get a bit of profile-by-association by wrapping the Carson article around another feature article on eco-minded paints.

Rachel Carson was *green* decades before anyone recognized the word as anything other than a color. And although she may not be a household name among our youth, they unknowingly witness the ever-lasting benefits of her work. In addition to fashion, my daughter enjoys lying on the sofa and reading sections of our provincial newspaper–*The Chronicle Herald*. The headline on page seven of an issue from the summer of 2009 read "Wolfville takes aim at lawn pesticides." It came complete with a picture of Wolfville's town mayor and a quote stating "We hoped this would become an election

---

[74] L. Lear and T. Woodham, "Rachel Carson: Environmental Champion," *Veranda*, April 2009.

issue."[75] Mayor Stead also recommended the use of natural products instead of synthetic chemicals to control weeds.

It is easy to dismiss Wolfville's mayor as the leader of a behind-the-times small town of no consequence, but not if you are familiar with it. Wolfville is home to one of Canada's top five undergraduate universities, and it received national attention by becoming the first Canadian town to ban smoking in vehicles carrying children. Wolfville is well educated and progressive, and if housing prices are an indicator, it is a desired place of residence.

From the pages of *The Chronicle Herald*, the town of Wolfville appears to be where Rachel Carson left us almost half a century ago. But anyone who visits this town in Annapolis Valley, and who strolls among its historic Acadian dykes, surrounding farmland, and the magnificent Cape Blomidon beyond, realizes it is not silent in spring.

Almost fifty years ago, Rachel Carson referenced this valley in the pages of *Silent Spring*. She identified the pest control approach taken by Nova Scotian entomologist A.D. Pickett, and she presented the Annapolis Valley's apple growers as a shining model to be emulated.[76]

The town of Wolfville is simply following in the footsteps of the small Quebec town of Hudson, which in 1991 implemented By-law 270, thereby prohibiting the use of pesticides with noted exceptions. Over a ten-year period, the chemical industry fought the town of Hudson, just as it fought Rachel Carson thirty years earlier. Industrial representatives took the Hudson battle all the way to the Supreme Court of Canada, and lost. By the time the Mayor Stead article appeared, there were province-wide bans on private use of

---

[75] G. Parker, "Wolfville Takes Aim at Lawn Pesticides," *Halifax (NS) Chronicle Herald,* June 8, 2009.
[76] Rachel Carson, *Silent Spring* (Boston: Houghton Mifflin, 1962), 225, 229-230.

lawn pesticides in both Quebec and Ontario, which collectively are home to the majority of Canada's population.

Rachel Carson's work remains incomplete, but by influencing the lives of a generation and their children, whether they realize it or not, she helped save us from our own destruction. Today, aspects of *Silent Spring* are dated, such as its extensive reference to DDT. Otherwise, the book continues to be a disturbing read and a rallying point for the Mayor Steads of the world.

Obviously, our understanding of the sea has advanced since Carson's publication of *The Sea Around Us*, but this book also continues to be relevant and in my opinion remains the most poetic account of the field of oceanography, albeit dated. In addition to identifying the need to take an ecosystem approach to managing the sea, Carson uses her poetic writing style to introduce us to its dynamics. She capitalized on our infatuation with the sea and its biology to unwittingly hook us on oceanography. No publication intended for a general audience has had as profound an effect upon my view of the sea as the combined effects of *The Sea Around Us* and *Silent Spring*.

Chapter Ten:

The Undersea World

Twenty years after he joined the French Navy, the stars had aligned for Jacques Cousteau. He was barely forty years old. Within a twelve month period, he evolved from French naval officer on a mine clearing and scuba research team to a forthcoming producer holding the makings of a blockbuster script.

There is another profound example of a person influencing our view of the sea by positioning his own view to be in the right place at the right time. Like Rachel Carson's view, it again surfaced in the midst of the twentieth century, but this additional view pertains to what lies *beneath* the sea, not what Carson saw from the shores of America.

Jacques-Yves Cousteau, his wife Simone, and fellow French explorers, contributed to the general public's late-twentieth century view of the sea by discovering the door to what lies beneath its surface. Cousteau showed us how we see the sea when we take the view of an explorer diving to and beyond the limits of visible light and human anatomy. He exceeded the boundaries of our common existence.

Cousteau and his fellow adventurers were the first to achieve these feats using emerging scuba technologies, and the first to bring them to the big screen and television as personal experiences. During those early days of scuba diving, they routinely risked their lives and everyone who sat in front of a screen or television realized what they were witnessing. It was captivating cinematography that influenced an entire generation.

Whether consciously or not, like others of this era, he filled the marine knowledge void with his own particular view of the sea. Unlike Rachel Carson's books, Jacques Cousteau's books, films and television programs do not teach marine biology, oceanography, or any other science. They teach us a few facts, but predominantly they provide adventure.

Cousteau was born in France in 1910, twelve years before my father entered this world on the Isle of Sheppey, across the English Channel from France. Like Edward Whitehouse, Jacques Cousteau was of modest ancestry and joined his country's navy at a young age. But they experienced different childhoods, had different reasons for joining the navy, and had fundamentally different views of the sea.

As a result of an astute career move by his father, as a lad Jacques travelled extensively while receiving a superior education and privileged upbringing. His youthful experiences led to strategic contacts and a sense of entrepreneurship, and eventually a novel vision of the sea. By realizing his vision, Cousteau became one of our greatest explorers. But even in his case, it all began with the navy.

His mother's ancestors were wine merchants, but Jacques Cousteau's father, Daniel, was the son of a village notary public. Daniel obtained a law degree and in 1906 became an advisor in Paris to the American millionaire James Hazen Hyde. The Cousteaus and their two sons, Pierre-Antoine and Jacques-Yves, accompanied Hyde as he travelled among Europe's high society.

After World War I, Daniel became the personal advisor to Eugene Higgins, then the wealthiest bachelor in New York City and an avid yachtsman. This introduced Jacques and his brother Pierre to boarding schools and a privileged view of the marine environment.

In 1920, Daniel's employment resulted in the family moving to New York for two years. There, the Cousteau boys learned to speak English and during summer camp at Lake Harvey, Vermont, teenaged Jacques initiated his passion for diving under water.

Upon the family's return to Paris with Higgins in 1922, Jacques bought one of the first home movie cameras available in France. He used it to produce and film amateur movie shorts, in which he was the screenwriter, lead actor, and director.

In 1929, when Edward Whitehouse was four years shy of entering the British naval academy at Holbrook, Jacques Cousteau graduated from school. One year later he joined the French Navy as a gunnery officer and for three years travelled widely, filming his adventures as he went. There used to be a saying–*join the navy and see the world*. Apparently, it has or at least *had* merit.

Eventually, Cousteau enrolled in the navy's aviation program and learned how to fly, but a severe injury sustained in a car accident in 1936 caused the French Navy to terminate his career as a pilot and assign him to the fleet in Toulon. Years later, Cousteau recognized this posting as a defining moment in his career and personal life. Like the rest of us, Jacques Cousteau's life was nonlinear, comprising a handful of defining moments punctuated by the rest of his life.

While stationed in Toulon, Cousteau met Lt. Philippe Tailliez and took up swimming to help with his post-accident physiotherapy. Here, he also dove underwater wearing goggles for the first time. While skin diving in 1938, he and Tailliez met a spear fisherman named Frédéric Dumas. Skin divers swim without the aid of an aqualung or other such assisted breathing apparatus. They use accessories such as mask, goggles, snorkel, fins, and spear gun. Skin diving and spear fishing have substantial roots in the Mediterranean in the 1930s; thus it is not surprising that in Dumas, Cousteau and Tailliez found an exceptional skin diver. Cousteau would later describe him as the best goggle diver in France, a man who could skin dive to an astounding sixty feet.

When war broke out in 1939, Jacques' father, Daniel Cousteau, was on the coast of England in Torquay, with his millionaire American employer Eugene Higgins. The Allies advised Higgins to stay put rather than try to sail his yacht out of England. As a result, he and Daniel remained in the United Kingdom for the duration of World War II. At the time, my father had just joined the Royal Navy and was stationed at naval barracks near Torquay. With only thirty-four miles of road separating them, my father and Jacques Cousteau's father were close enough to dine together, but I doubt Higgins and Daniel Cousteau dined with seventeen-year-old apprentice engine room artificers.

From the perspective of developing his diving career and the western world's subsequent view of the sea, it is fortunate that Jacques Cousteau was not trapped in the United Kingdom with his father when war broke out. If he had, he may not have benefited from the connections of his wife, Simone Melchior, and therefore never have co-invented the aqualung.

Jacques met Simone in France in 1936, when she was seventeen and he twenty six, a shocking age differential by today's western standards. They married after a one-year, long distance courtship, largely via pen, paper and post. Simone was the daughter of a former naval officer and her family tree included three generations of admirals, but according to her husband she grew up in a convent in Japan. In her, Cousteau found a young woman ready for serious adventure, and a well-connected companion who later would be the mother of his two sons.

I doubt she is recognized as such, but Simone Melchior was the first female to scuba dive with the aqualung, and the only woman to sail on every major voyage of the *Calypso*–Cousteau's famed vessel. But according to her husband, she did not develop his enthusiasm for diving. Apparently, as would be expected with her naval relatives and ancestors, she spent a good deal of her life on the sea but not in it. At the time she would also have endured the then widely-held naval superstition regarding women on board while at sea. Based on his observations of Simone, and Dumas' lack of fan mail from the opposite sex, in his book *The Silent World* Cousteau concludes that women are suspicious of diving.

Society often underrates the woman behind the man, but from the standpoint of pushing forth the frontiers of ocean observing, Simone's greatest tangible contribution to Jacques Cousteau's definitive view of the sea was putting him in contact with her father. In addition to having senior naval connections, Monsieur Melchior was an executive with a French company that produced industrial gases. Founded in 1902, Air Liquide eventually grew into a global corporate empire with forty-three thousand employees in seventy-five countries.

As was the case with his father, Jacques' father-in-law provided connections of profound influence. Cousteau, Tailliez, and Dumas realized the need for compressed air to stay down longer during their diving adventures. They experimented with underwater breathing equipment provided to them by the French Navy, including the Le Prieur breathing device, re-breathing technology and the Fernez pump. But they lacked an automated open-valve design that allowed them to breathe in from a self-regulated pressurized tank and then exhale into the water through the same mouthpiece.

At Air Liquide in Paris, Cousteau's father-in-law put him in contact with company engineer Émile Gagnan, who was experimenting with the use of gas as an alternative to petrol for the common automobile. This happened in December 1942, during the height of World War II, in occupied France, while Cousteau was still an officer in the then incapacitated French Navy. Gagnan showed Cousteau a prototype of the valve he had engineered for such purpose. With his father-in-law a director of the company, Cousteau convinced Air Liquide to co-develop an underwater breathing apparatus based on Gagnan's valve and Cousteau's knowledge, and to finance the work.

Cousteau and Gagnan tested the first prototype that Gagnan designed for breathing underwater in a river on the outskirts of Paris, with Gagnan and Simone Melchior, now Mrs. Cousteau, standing on the bank. They tested the next version in a tank in Gagnan's lab in

Paris. Neither Tailliez nor Dumas were present for these Paris-based developments, but during the following summer, together with Jacques and Simone, they tested the device during hundreds of dives in the Mediterranean. They also filmed their adventures using a second-hand camera sealed in an underwater housing built by a colleague in the navy.

In their joint patent application that year, Gagnan and Cousteau referred to their diving device as an "aqualung", and thus began a profound influence upon my perception of the sea and apparently that of countless others. Just this morning I was reminded of this influence when my teenage daughter almost ruined my breakfast. She gasped in disgust while drinking fresh, cool orange juice my wife had just purchased. I thought she had swallowed a cockroach or something, but it turned out my wife had bought the wrong brand. She had bought juice with pulp instead of without. My daughter's behavior demonstrated the extent to which our youth take food for granted and it caused me to remember the first day Jacques Cousteau tested a properly functioning version of the aqualung. It happened in 1943, when France was occupied by the Germans and Italians. The basics of life were in such short supply that Jacques, Simone, and their children shared a Mediterranean villa in the village of Bandol with the Tailliez family, Dumas, and a fellow sailor and his wife, as a means of pooling resources. The villa had a small vegetable patch; otherwise, the entire household lived largely on a diet of beans and their allotted rations of bread and butter, some days for breakfast, lunch and supper. During the war people often went to bed hungry or starving, in France and elsewhere in Europe.

Publicly, Cousteau is credited for inventing the aqualung, but it is based on a valve designed and built by Gagnan, who subsequently redesigned and rebuilt the valve based on field tests performed first by Cousteau and later by Cousteau, Tailliez, and Dumas. The morning after Gagnan shipped Cousteau what subsequently became the first functioning version of the aqualung,

Cousteau and his housemates walked to the beach to give the instrument its inaugural live test. From his first breath, Cousteau was delighted with the results. In his biography of the French adventurer, Brad Matsen states that on this first dive, Cousteau dove to a maximum depth of sixty feet, stood on the bottom at thirty feet, somersaulted, flipped, barrel rolled and laughed so hard he lost his mouthpiece. His three tanks of air allowed sixty minutes at sixty feet; but the water was cold, thus heat loss became another limiting factor.[77]

Before heading in, Cousteau decided to do something he did not dare as a free diver, out of fear of being trapped. He entered a narrow and dimly lit underwater tunnel. When his tanks scrapped the walls of the tunnel, however, he decided to go no further. He rolled on his back to make his exit and then looked up at the ceiling of the tunnel. It was crawling with lobsters, hundreds of them. As Cousteau backed out of the tunnel he grabbed two of the tasty delicacies, and then returned five more times that day. Thus, subsistence fishing became the first application of scuba diving. Of course fishing via aqualung did not become a national pastime because a scuba diver consumes a considerable amount of energy while diving. As Cousteau noted, you have to be careful not to spend more energy than the prey provides.

I recited this story to my recovering daughter, who refused to drink her orange juice. She showed genuine interest and was touched by its message, but as noted by Monty Python, if you tell that story to the average kid today, they won't believe you. Obviously, the French adventurers not only survived the period but went on to experiment with techniques and gear that allowed them to dive deeper and stay down longer. In the months, years, and decades that followed, Dumas became the first human to take the aqualung to two hundred feet and

---

[77] B. Matsen, *Jacques Cousteau: The Sea King* (New York: Pantheon Books, 2009), 58-61, 63.

beyond. He was also the subject of Cousteau's first underwater movie short, and he helped Cousteau write his break-out 1953 book, *The Silent World*. Although not common knowledge, after the war Émile Gagnan emigrated to Canada in search of a better life, just like my parents. In Montreal, he worked for the Canadian subsidiary of Air Liquide, and he set up the division that became the inaugural North American manufacturer of the aqualung, with the company owning ninety-nine percent of its shares and Cousteau the remaining one percent.[78]

In *The Silent World*, his first of more than fifty books, Cousteau states they tested the aqualung in a concealed cove and that the Italians gave them a hard time while skin diving. Seeing skin divers on a Mediterranean beach holding spears and fish would be innocuous enough to a German or Italian patrol guard, but what about Cousteau, Dumas, or Tailliez emerging from the water wearing an aqualung, while carrying an underwater camera? Biographer Richard Munson states that Cousteau did not attempt to conceal his equipment from the Germans and Italians, who viewed him as a "harmless eccentric".[79] By the time World War II broke out, the Germans were certainly manufacturing dive gear, albeit not the aqualung, and both sides deployed frogmen during the war.

Near the end of 1944, Cousteau went to England to present the aqualung to the Allies and to propose its use for military purposes, but they did not bite. By then, like the Germans and Italians they possessed underwater breathing or re-breathing equipment, but not the aqualung. In 1937, for example, fellow Frenchman Georges Commeinhes, who died during the liberation of Europe in 1944, developed an open-circuit regulator which he offered to the French Navy in 1939. Like the sound and transducer scientists of Alexander Graham Bell's era, Commeinhes almost got it right. He was

---

[78] Ibid., 92.
[79] Munson, *Cousteau: The Captain and His World*, 32.

experimenting in a field whose time had come. It is likely that the acronym *scuba*, which stands for *self-contained underwater breathing apparatus*, was coined by the Allies sometime around World War II, not by Cousteau or any member of the French team. The military version would have been classified at the time. An Internet search attributes the term to the US Navy circa 1939, in association with re-breathing technology that mixes exhaled breath with oxygen. This technique has the advantage of being covert as it does not emit bubbles. Cousteau experimented with this type of gear, prior to developing the aqualung with Émile Gagnan, but he almost died while testing it. Re-breathing gear is not a recreational technology.

Axel Madsen, a Cousteau biographer, first mentions the *scuba* acronym while discussing Cousteau's 1944 visit to the Allies in England. The public did not adopt it until many years after Cousteau took the technology outside of France. After the war, Cousteau and his colleagues continued to refer to the technology as the aqualung, as did the American and British public. The 27 November 1950 issue of *Life* magazine, for example, calls the activity free diving and the breathing device the "Aqua-lung".[80] In her 13 May 1956 *New York Times* book review of James Dugan's *Underwater Explorers*, Rachel Carson also refers to the device as the aqualung. The following year, *New York Times* writer Clarence Lovejoy advised that the acronym *scuba* had been coined, while still referring to the apparatus itself as the aqualung in the remainder of his article. He refers to this in connection with an observation that underwater exploring is a naval intelligence activity.

In the US, the term *free diving* lingered into 1960, with *Time* magazine using both *free diving* and *scuba* interchangeably in a feature article on Cousteau. Common terminology may have evolved in the US, from aqualung to scuba, much in the way people now refer

---

[80] "Photographic Essay Underwater Wonders," *Life,* November 27, 1950, 119.

to a tissue rather than a Kleenex©. Cousteau's recognition and promotion of the brand he patented with Air Liquide is evident throughout his 1963 book, *The Living Sea*. Although released years after the American public adopted the term scuba, the word *scuba* does not appear anywhere within the book and Cousteau no longer refers to the aqualung per se. He refers to it by Air Liquide's commercial brand name–Aqua-Lung©.

The Allies did not accept the aqualung during Cousteau's 1944 visit to England, but after the occupation of France, Cousteau showed one of his underwater short films to the French Navy. It convinced them to commission Tailliez and Cousteau, both of whom were still in the navy, to use the technology to search for underwater mines and to establish an undersea naval research group. Thus, it was Cousteau's film, not the technology itself, that secured critical development funding and led to the equipment's first practical application–underwater military operations.

As the senior officer in charge of the research group, Tailliez hired Dumas and other navy personnel were brought on board and taught how to scuba dive. In addition to mine surveying, their orders included studying the physiology of freestyle diving, which became another accomplishment of the team. But they also worked on underwater vehicles, lights, and other equipment and brought scientists along on navy-backed cruises to study the Mediterranean itself. It all began with post-war clearing of German mines for the French Navy, and it was all funded by the military.

In his first book, Cousteau refers to using "a factory-new aqualung" in October of 1943, but Air Liquide did not begin producing the device commercially until after the war, in 1946. In the same year, Cousteau's underwater black and white film *Épaves* (sunken ships), which had been showing in Parisian theatres since the city was liberated in 1944, won a short-film award at the newly formed Cannes film festival. At the age of thirty six, twenty years before The American Broadcasting Company (ABC) picked up his underwater television series, Cousteau became an entrepreneur and film celebrity in his own country.

Jacques Cousteau passed through California once in 1932, while returning home from a cruise with the French Navy, but his prime time debut with the American public came in 1950 when *Life* magazine published an article on him, featuring photographs of underwater adventures. Actually, his American print-media debut was two years previous in a smaller circulation and somewhat technical publication called *Science Illustrated.* The article was written by James Dugan, who Cousteau had met in England in 1944. Previously, Dugan had sent his story to major editors in Europe and America, but they all rejected it. The article in *Life* was the first major American print-media exposure for Cousteau. It came about as a result of a *Life* magazine editor attending a New York screening of short films brought back from Europe by a cultural attaché who worked for the United Nations.[81]

Most of the *Life* magazine photographs are of Dumas, as Cousteau was behind the camera. But unmistakably, the text that accompanies the seven-page photo spread profiles Cousteau, not the French naval team he worked with. The article references more than one thousand dives in the Mediterranean and Atlantic, yet it devotes two of its seven pages and five of its fourteen photos to a single shark, with one of the grainy but novel black and white photographs showing Dumas reaching out to touch the beast. With a circulation in excess of five million in 1950, *Life* knew how to sell magazines and in the process, inadvertently or otherwise, they also sold Cousteau to the American public.

Despite his modest ancestry, the magazine article describes Cousteau as "well-bred" and having "worked under the very noses of the Nazis". It does not credit the two colleagues who also risked their lives. Instead, it credits Cousteau for inventing the aqualung and the

---

[81] Matsen, *Jacques Cousteau*, 102-103.

underwater camera he used to take the photos. No mention of Simone, Émile Gagnan, Air Liquide, or fabricators at the French Navy docks. No mention of the fact that Philippe Tailliez was in charge of the underwater research unit or that he shot one of the team's early underwater movies using a Pathé camera sealed in a fruit jar. It even refers to the French Navy team as Cousteau's men. This approach was consistent with that taken by James Dugan two years previous, in which he referred to "Cousteau's divers" and credits him for inventing a new species Dugan calls "menfish".

I doubt Jacques Cousteau had anything to do with writing the brief amount of text that accompanied the *Life* magazine photos. It was written in English, not French, and when does the interviewer allow the interviewee to write their article? In this case, *Life* does not credit anyone for writing the text. The article is simply entitled *Photographic Essay*, names divers that appear in photos, and Cousteau for having taken them. In the American version of his 1953 book *The Silent World,* Cousteau clearly identifies himself as the co-inventor of the aqualung, but the deed was done. Like the discovered rock band whose lead singer gets the record deal, the die was cast as a team of one. Just one week after this article appeared across America, Universal Pictures obtained the rights to Cousteau's short films and thereafter started showing them as shorts in the cinemas of the United States.

Although some of the photos had appeared in the previous *Science Illustrated* article, this 1950 *Life* photo essay is likely the first time such photos were seen by the American public-at-large, and Universal Pictures picked up Cousteau's film rights as a result of having seen the article in *Life*. The photos appeared again among the pages of Cousteau's 1953 book, *The Silent World*. By 1960, this book enjoyed worldwide sales of five million copies and it received great reviews upon its release in English in the United Kingdom in 1952. The British press based their comments on the book and therefore presented a broader view than *Life* magazine. *The Sunday Times,* for example, recognized the French underwater research group, the French Navy, and also Dumas for co-writing the book.[82]

Jacques Cousteau's 1950 profile in *Life* magazine was his American coming-out party, but for Rachel Carson, having her work published in this renowned magazine was one of many accolades she received in the United States as a result of her break-out book, *The Sea Around Us*. In 1953, the same year Jacques Cousteau published *The Silent World* in the United States, a film based on *The Sea Around Us* won the Academy Award for best documentary, three years before Cousteau won the same award in the same category for the film version of his book.

Their formative years overlapped, but I have found no evidence that Carson's view of the sea was significantly influenced by Jacques Cousteau's, or vice versa. Carson's view was based on personal experiences on the eastern shores of the United States, scientific literature, public reports, professional conversations, and personal correspondence. By the time she died, Carson knew Cousteau very well.[83] But when she started to write *The Sea Around Us* in the summer of 1946, and when she experienced her only adventure under water in 1949, it is possible that she had not even heard of Jacques Cousteau.

Carson submitted *The Sea Around Us* manuscript five months before Cousteau was introduced to America in *Life* magazine in November 1950. Her book makes no reference to his work and states: "Only two men in all the history of the world have had the experience of descending, alive, beyond the range of visible light."[84] She then acknowledges the use of the bathysphere by William Beebe and Otis

---

[82] *Sunday Times*, March 28, 1953 (author not specified, but likely Ian Fleming).
[83] Linda Lear, author of *Rachel Carson*, personal communication.
[84] Rachel Carson, *The Sea Around Us* (New York: Oxford University Press, 1951), 38.

Burton. In the same book she also states: "But we know now that the conception of the sea as a silent place is wholly false."[85]

Carson published this sentence two years before Jacques Cousteau published his award-winning best seller, *The Silent World*. Cousteau's title, of course, refers to what he experienced as a scuba diver. This raises the question of whose concept she was referring to. If she understood the sea to produce sound, then why make the statement?

David Dempsey picked up on Carson's statement in his 1951 *New York Times* review of *The Sea Around Us*, for significant reason.[86] With this statement, Rachel Carson refers to the fact that by the time her book was published, hydrophone networks had been embedded in the sea by the US Navy, as a component of its antisubmarine warfare acoustics program. During this period, oceanographic institutions, such as the one frequented by Carson, were also using civilian or otherwise declassified acoustic technologies to investigate sounds made by marine animals. Shrimp, for example, generate detectable sounds. In addition to the submarines they searched for, military installations detected such sounds plus those made by ships and other marine structures. A key issue in this area is whether non-indigenous sound impacts marine life, and if so to what extent. Although first raised in the 1970s, the marine community has yet to come to universal conclusion on the subject.[87] Regardless, in 1951 Rachel Carson disclosed with clarity where it all started:

"One very common misconception about the sea was corrected by studies made during the Second World War. We always used to think of the deep sea as a place of silence....When Navy technicians began

---

[85] Ibid., 51.

[86] D. Dempsey, "Books of the Times," *New York Times*, July 2, 1951.

[87] Gotz et al., *Overview of the Impacts of Anthropogenic Underwater Sound in the Marine Environment* (London: OSPAR Commission, 2009), 10.

listening for submarines during the war, they heard a most extraordinary uproar."[88]

The fact that Carson concluded in 1951 that the sea is not silent indicates she had access to marine acoustic transducer data at an early stage of its operational application. Her book even references data collected in 1942 by a US Navy hydrophone network installed in Chesapeake Bay, during World War II.

During its war-time development, this technology and its resulting data would have been classified. My father chose not to write about his wartime naval experiences, but Carson seems to have written about hers. She was never in the navy but she comprehended its scientific accomplishments and synthesized them with poetic style. Just as Rudyard Kipling influenced our perception of the "seven seas" with his poetry in 1896, Carson did it in 1951 but through application of poetic techniques rather than through publication of poetry per se. Her ability to present complicated subjects to the general public was recognized in both *New York Times* reviews of *The Sea Around Us*.[89] Both also recognize the book as being one of oceanography, not biology.

Like all significant navies, the US Navy maintains a classified maritime acoustic technology program that continues to evade the public's view of the sea. This is why my father's advice about not joining the navy also applies to engineers and scientists who aspire to be recognized as great inventors. In the military, you may discover great inventions, but you will not be able to talk about it.

Consider the sinking of the *Titanic* in 1912. It inspired a patent application just five days thereafter by the British inventor L.F. Richardson, who proposed the use of echo ranging as a means to

---

[88] Lear, ed., *Lost Woods: The Discovered Writing of Rachel Carson*, 82.
[89] Dempsey, "Books of the Times,"; and J.N. Leonard, "And His Wonders in the Deep: A Scientist Draws an Intimate Portrait of the Winding Sea and its Churning Life," *New York Times*, July 1, 1951.

detect icebergs. Unfortunately for Richardson, suitable acoustic transducers were not available until about 1914 when a Canadian working in the United States, R.A. Fessenden, developed a moving coil transducer. It was demonstrated for its application to ice detection, but also for communicating between submarines. To professionals working in this field, it became known as the Fessenden oscillator.

However, with World War I in view, underwater acoustics quickly moved into the naval intelligence realm as French and British researchers, backed by their respective navies, laid the foundations for marine acoustics and modern antisubmarine warfare. Practical application also proceeded in the United States with numerous arrays of hydrophone listening devices installed and Fessenden oscillators deployed on American submarines.[90]

Today, there are as many acoustic sensors on boats as telephones, but unlike the telephone, the public does not associate this invention with anyone in particular.

Jacques Cousteau's first public reference to the concept of a silent sea was in 1944 in his short French film *Paysages du Silence* (*Landscapes of Silence*). This film was referenced in the November 1950 *Life* magazine article on Cousteau, but again, this article appeared after Carson submitted *The Sea Around Us* to her publisher.

Carson had certainly heard of Cousteau by 1953, as the outside jacket cover of Cousteau's *The Silent World* features commentary by Carson. But in 1956, when she reviewed James Dugan's book for *The New York Times*, she recognized the Scripps Institution of Oceanography in California as having the largest group of scientific divers. Her only reference to Cousteau comes in the final paragraph of her review, which focuses on the short lifespan of new

---

[90] C.H. Sherman and J.L. Butler, *Transducers and Arrays for Underwater Sound* (New York: Springer, 2007), 4.

inventions. She quotes Cousteau as having described his aqualung as "primitive and unworthy of contemporary levels of science."[91]

In her 1960 preface to the revised edition of *The Sea Around Us*, in which she describes significant advances in the field to date, Carson again makes no reference to Jacques Cousteau, his colleagues, their work, or scuba diving. His name does appear twice in the back material of the revised edition. In an appendix reference to Auguste Piccard's bathyscaphe, Carson notes Piccard and Cousteau co-directed the construction of Piccard's second generation submarine; and in her list of suggested readings she references *The Silent World* and describes it as a fascinating read, as she did in her original 1953 commentary on the book.

These observations may simply reflect the fact that in the revised edition Carson chose not to modify the original body of text and instead add material to the back of the book, but it may also reflect a lack of recognition of Cousteau's work within the marine science community. He was not trained as a scientist and did not publish in peer-reviewed science journals, whereas Carson's most famous books are based on review of scientific literature and reports. It appears that she enjoyed reading his book, but because it was beyond the scope of marine science, it did not feature even in the revised edition of *The Sea Around Us*.

Regardless, Jacques Cousteau and Rachel Carson have something in common when it comes to their views of the sea. There are high profile exceptions, but substantive discovery in oceanography is associated with periods of war and the research arms of formidable navies, either directly or indirectly through naval research funding to civilian scientists. In other words, marine science percolated along until the outbreak of World War II; then it entered its heyday.

---

[91] Rachel Carson, "Underwater Explorers," *New York Times,* May 13, 1956.

Rachel Carson was a civilian throughout World War II, and with certainty she was not a research scientist. But she appears to have had insider knowledge on oceanographic technologies developed in support of the war. Prior to attending Johns Hopkins in 1929, Carson made the first of several visits to the Woods Hole Marine Biological Laboratory, Massachusetts, where she immersed herself in marine studies and made valuable contacts. This period is noteworthy as the now renowned Woods Hole Oceanographic Institution came into being the year after her first visit. By the time Carson's multiple visits to Woods Hole had familiarized her with its facilities and activities, the US Navy had established significant influence on campus, particularly within the disciplines of marine acoustics, physics, and geophysics. It is not by accident that theoretical acousticians like Frederick Hunt came into their US faculty positions. Science requires funding and no one funds marine science like the US Navy.

Cousteau visited the United States again in 1952, the same year *The Silent World* was released in the United Kingdom. During this trip he inaugurated what would become an extensive relationship with the National Geographic Society, furthered his relationship with the American writer James Dugan, and signed a film production contract with CBS, his first with an American television station.

In the same year that he was profiled in *Life* magazine, Cousteau purchased his famed research vessel *Calypso*, with funding provided by the British philanthropist Thomas Loël Guinness, whom he and Simone first met in a bar in Auron during World War II.[92] The purchase happened after Cousteau requested a term leave from active military duty. Built in 1942 in Seattle, Washington, for the British Royal Navy, *Calypso* sailed from France on its maiden voyage as Cousteau's ship in 1951.

---

[92] Munson, *Cousteau: The Captain and His World*, 65.

Through an Irish grandmother, Jacques' wife Simone was also the cousin of Sir Basil Jackson, the head of British Petroleum in the 1950s. In 1954, a subsidiary of British Petroleum saved the *Calypso* from running out of money by chartering the vessel and its crew for petroleum exploration work. Cousteau's 1963 account of the event states that his 1953 book led the subsidiary's representative to the *Calypso*, not Simone's family connections. Regardless, twenty years after he joined the French Navy, the stars had aligned for Jacques Cousteau. He was barely forty years old. Within a twelve month period, he evolved from French naval officer on a mine clearing and scuba research team to a forthcoming producer holding the makings of a blockbuster script.

In 1956 Cousteau took Cannes again with his first full-length movie *Le Monde du Silence.* It was released in America with the same name as his book, *The Silent World,* and won the Academy Award that year for best feature documentary, Cousteau's first.[93] Uncommon at the time, the film was in color. One biographer described it as "... one hour and twenty-seven minutes of marvel and thrills"[94] while another said it ignited "imagination and sense of wonder as never before."[95]

Cousteau surfaced from it all as an international celebrity, but due to the nature of his work his face was not yet recognizable to the American public. Thus, when he appeared on the popular American television program *What's My Line,* in September 1956, the learned panel did not recognize him or his voice, but to the home audience he was introduced as the "world's foremost underwater explorer".

The Silent World and various short and feature films had already made Cousteau an international celebrity by the time he sailed

[93] In 1964, Cousteau's second feature film–*World Without Sun* won the Academy Award for best feature documentary.
[94] A. Madsen, *Cousteau: An Unauthorized Biography* (New York: Beaufort Books, 1986), 97-98.
[95] Munson, *Cousteau: The Captain and His World*, 16.

Calypso into New York harbor in 1959, but the pinnacle of his success as an American celebrity came when ABC agreed to pay four million dollars for the production of twelve inaugurating one-hour color television episodes of *The Undersea World of Jacques Cousteau*. The show ran from 1968 until 1976, with a total of thirty-six episodes. By the time the multi-Emmy award winning show ended, *Calypso* had sailed on four of Earth's five oceans–all but the Arctic.

Within months of winning his first Academy Award, Cousteau resigned from the French Navy altogether. Like my father, Cousteau joined the sea of servicemen who left the militaries of Europe after World War II; innumerable survivors believing a change is as good as a vacation. From the perspective of how we view the sea, Cousteau stands out among them. By spring of 1960, he was on the cover of *Time* magazine, as the undisputed figurehead for a scuba diving community comprising two hundred thousand divers within the United States, and three hundred and fifty thousand worldwide.

Unlike my father, when Jacques Cousteau left Europe's post-war navy, he did not move to North America for more military life. Coincidentally, he followed the two pieces of fatherly advice I recalled in 1976 on the docks of Esquimalt harbor. Cousteau left the French Navy and changed direction, frequently. According to the biographer Axel Madsen, Cousteau never took vacations because they imply "a change of activity", which Cousteau was always doing anyway.

Although he spent a large part of his post-war life in the United States, Cousteau did not actually move there. In 1957, he became director of Monaco's Oceanographic Museum, where he maintained an office for decades, while travelling extensively.

The public views Cousteau as a marine adventurer and explorer who filmed the biology of the sea, but the average person does not differentiate between marine biology and biological oceanography. Aspects of Cousteau's view linger today. He is, for example, the reason why many people think oceanographers scuba dive, even though marine science has progressed far beyond what can be gained through application of scuba gear and marine cinematography. Marine biologists are renowned for scuba diving, but a biological oceanographer could spend their time ashore pondering computer-based models and physical processes that influence ecosystems. Like Rachel Carson, it is possible to have a biological oceanographer who neither scuba dives, nor fond of swimming, nor goes to sea on a regular basis.

Although documentary in their approach, Cousteau's films and television series deliberately aimed for our hearts and imaginations, not our brains, just like theatre. Cousteau once told reporters he had an intense dislike for the word documentary, and that neither of his first two feature-length films taught fact. He noted, for example, that in his Oscar winning feature film *World Without Sun*, they didn't even identify the locale as the Red Sea.[96] And this was not lost on public opinion of the time. In his 30 September 1956 *New York Times* review of Cousteau's feature film *The Silent World*, Bosley Crowther wrote: "exactly what Captain Cousteau learned for the benefit of oceanographic science and for our National Geographic Society is not explained."[97] But in the same article he also observed: "However, his voyaging turned up a beautiful and absorbing nature film, and that is enough for anybody whose scientific interest does not range very far outside a theatre."

---

[96] Ibid., 134.
[97] B. Crowther, "The Real Things," *New York Times,* September 30, 1956.

Chapter Eleven:

Oh James

The man with the golden typewriter stood next to the world's greatest underwater explorer. The typewritten pages that followed continue to influence our view of the sea, more than half a century after they were written.

In 1958, *New York Times* writer Rita Reif describes scuba diving much as it is known today, routinely referring to it in an article on skin diving equipment for sale at Macy's. But in his 1961 James Bond book, *Thunderball*, British author Ian Fleming continues to refer to the device as the aqualung and the act itself as aqualunging. Although the two writers addressed the same subject, they had different views of it.

Of the two views, Fleming's stands out. He was born in the United Kingdom one year after Rachel Carson and two before Jacques Cousteau. Two of them joined the navy, but got out while they were still young, and all three proved my father's advice that a change is as good as a vacation. In so doing, all three used the experiences of one career to become famous in another. Decades before the invention of the Internet, cell phone, and satellite television, from separate countries they delivered their personal views of the sea to a global audience. With seeming independence, they founded the mid-twentieth century view of the sea.

Like Jacques Cousteau, Ian Fleming grew up in an environment of wealth, boarding schools and family connections. Unlike Cousteau, he did not thrive in it. Fleming spent time at Eton, but unlike his older brother did not move on to Oxford, or any other

English university. His mother decided a fashionable officer's commission was a suitable alternative and enrolled him at Sandhurst, Britain's famed military school. But he resigned from Sandhurst, reportedly after contracting a sexually transmitted disease during a one-night stand in Soho.[98] Instead, Fleming immersed himself in books and languages. He studied the Russian language, became fluent in German and French, and eventually established a book collection of considerable value that focused on "great scientific discoveries of the nineteenth century".[99] He even had a copy of Madame Currie's doctorate thesis. After another failed attempt at a fashionable English career, this time with the Foreign Office, his family used its connections again to land him a probationary journalist position at Reuters, the then British-owned news agency.

Fleming's mother did not view journalism as fashionable, but it proved to be his defining moment, and lucky break. At Reuters he got his first experience in the world of espionage and his first opportunity to publish on the subject. In the 1930s, Russia arrested several British nationals working for an electrical company in Russia, and put them on trial for commercial espionage. This caught the attention of the British government and media. Reuters dispatched Fleming to Moscow to cover the trial first hand.

He enjoyed the work, but a journalist's salary was not for Fleming. With the family's wealth locked out of reach in wills and trusts, he started working in the financial sector. The Fleming family owned a merchant bank, Robert Fleming & Co., thus the connection to a field in which he had no formal training or hands-on experience. It was during this short-lived financial career, however, that Ian Fleming met Rear-Admiral John Godfrey, who had just been appointed Britain's director of naval intelligence. As such, Godfrey

---

[98] Lycett, *Ian Fleming: The Man Behind James Bond*, 28.
[99] J. Pearson, *The Life of Ian Fleming* (London: Companion Book Club, 1966), 82.

reported to the first lord of the admiralty, which at the time was Winston Churchill. In July 1939, at the age of 31, Fleming became Godfrey's personal assistant within Britain's renowned Special Branch, which focused on naval intelligence and marine meteorology. The jump from banker and stockbroker to naval intelligence was not, however, a matter of money. His coverage of the Russian spy trial, as a reporter for Reuters, generated connections within Britain's Foreign Office. The resulting file on Fleming probably acknowledged his diverse skills, including command of certain foreign languages. Also, during the previous spring, while he was still a stockbroker, Ian Fleming was mysteriously seconded to the London *Times* and sent back to Russia, this time to cover a trade mission to Moscow. According to an article published in *Pravda*, Fleming participated in the mission as a spy for British Intelligence.[100]

As Godfrey's personal assistant, Fleming occupied a desk in the now legendary Room 39, and wore a naval uniform assigned to the Royal Naval Volunteer Reserve.[101] Godfrey had the office next door, Winston Churchill was one floor up, and the private entrance to No. 10 Downing Street was on the opposite side of the square. Fleming started as a lieutenant, but as he regularly interacted with high-ranking officials, Godfrey soon promoted him to the rank of commander, with a short stint in between as a lieutenant commander. Unlike Jacques Cousteau and Edward Whitehouse, Commander Fleming became a naval officer instantaneously. This did not go unnoticed by teasing acquaintances, who called him the "Chocolate Sailor", in reference to a Black Magic chocolates advertisement that was running at the time.

World War II broke out two months after Fleming joined Britain's Special Branch and what followed was no box of chocolates.

---

[100] Ibid., 91.
[101] D. McLachlan, *Room 39: A Study in Naval Intelligence* (New York: Atheneum, 1968).

The war and the navy did, however, make the man. The experience Commander Fleming gained as a naval intelligence officer generated ideas that subsequently became the life of Commander Bond, including the ever present connection between British and American intelligence. Fleming did not, however, incorporate the fact that the intelligence branch he served also handled coastal environmental intelligence.

The diffuse transition between fact and fiction is evident in the behind-the-scenes documentary on the production of the Bond movie *Thunderball*. A member of the production crew tells the story of a telephone call he received from someone claiming to be a military captain with the Royal Engineers. The officer was enquiring about the miniaturized underwater re-breathing apparatus used by Bond in the movie. It was a prop, not a functional piece of kit, and the caller hung up upon obtaining this information. This tidbit of British cinematography is misleading as the militaries of the day most certainly led the development of game-changing oceanographic technologies. They did not follow.

On occasion, James Bond wore a commander's uniform without any indication of having served time on the grey ships, just like the author himself. Fleming did hitch a ride home to England once on one of His Majesty's war ships. He boarded HMS *London* in December 1943 when it was ashore in Gibraltar, the same port in which Edward Whitehouse disembarked from the same ship in 1949. My father was aboard her when she sailed up the Yangtze River in late April, 1949, in an attempt to rescue the converted frigate HMS *Amethyst*. He was one of the lucky ones when he disembarked from her decks the following August in Gibraltar. There could not have been a greater contrast between my father's experience on HMS *London* and Fleming's.

Six months after Edward Whitehouse joined her crew, HMS *London* sailed from England to the South China Sea, right into a civil war. The British cruiser had recently received an extensive refit, all ready for what would become its final deployment and deadliest service. Mao Tse-tung's Communists were challenging the rule of China's Nationalists, with force. The Communists shelled HMS *Amethyst* as she was sailing up the Yangtze River, causing extensive damage that left the ship out of control. After running aground at Rose Island, with the Nationalists on one side of the river and the Communists on the other but preparing to cross, the British frigate radioed for help.

HMS *Consort* sailed down river from Nanking to assist. Although a British destroyer, being confined by the river she became the proverbial sitting duck. With casualties, and her wheelhouse destroyed, the *Consort* abandoned the rescue and continued down river to Kiang Yin, where she anchored alongside HMS *London* and HMS *Black Swan*.

What followed became naval history, subsequently immortalized in the 1957 movie entitled *Battle Hell*. The *London's* commanding officer, Captain Peter Cazalet, lost thirteen sailors on the Yangtze, plus more than fifty wounded, but he did not rescue the *Amethyst*. Having sustained severe shell damage to his ship, he realized that continuing the rescue attempt was suicide. The wheel was ordered hard to starboard and the engine room full astern on starboard engine.

In addition to the engines themselves, the *London's* guns, and the Communists' piercing shells, that order likely consumed my father's view of the sea that day. With the ship's bridge shattered by a bursting overhead shell and its pilots dead or unconscious, the engine room turned a naval cruiser doing twenty knots while under fire in a river no more than a mile wide. The sight from shore must have been gobsmacking.

Two months after my father arrived in Gibraltar on HMS *London*, Mao Tse-tung stood before the gates of the Forbidden City and announced the inauguration of his new regime. Mao's forces had shelled the *London* again during its trip back down river. The beating

162

sustained by the ship and its crew was so brutal that the ship was sold for scrap upon its return to England.

HMS *Amethyst* broke free of her Yangtze prison on her own accord on 31 July. After the Yangtze incident, Captain Peter Cazalet continued his career in the Royal Navy, eventually receiving a knighthood and attaining the rank of Vice Admiral. For his services in the Royal Navy, Edward Whitehouse received the 1939-45 Star, the Atlantic, Africa, and Burma Stars, the France and Germany clasp, the War Medal of 1949, and in June 1951, the Naval General Service Medal with Yangtze Bar.

When Commander Ian Fleming arrived home on HMS *London,* he described the trip as "a millionaire's Mediterranean cruise."[102] When Engine Room Artificer Edward Whitehouse arrived home on the *London,* it had hammocks stuffed in shell holes in the ship's hull, to keep it afloat.[103] On the *London,* both Fleming and Whitehouse sailed the seas from the same port to the same country on the same ship, but they obtained completely different views of the sea. After HMS *London* returned to England from China, Edward Whitehouse never sailed again for the Royal Navy. Although he survived what some recall in glorious terms, he never spoke as such.

After the war, like Edward Whitehouse, Ian Fleming did not stay in the Royal Navy, but unlike Whitehouse he did not join another. The war had ended but Fleming remained a member of an affluent family. He was not limited by the confines of a common life, which in Edward's case included the lack of a decent formal education.

Ian Fleming started writing his James Bond novels after he left British intelligence at the end of World War II. He wrote them at his famed seaside house in Jamaica, which he called *Goldeneye,* the

---

[102] Lycett, *Ian Fleming: The Man Behind James Bond*, 150.
[103] I. Ballantyne, *H.M.S. London: Warships of the Royal Navy* (Barnsley: Leo Cooper, 2003), 148.

code name for one of the intelligence operations he worked on during the war, although there are other suggested inspirations for the name. While in Jamaica, he pinched the name *James Bond* from his copy of the *Birds of the West Indies*.[104] Bond was a real-life zoologist who specialized in birds. At Goldeneye, in addition to watching birds, writing fiction, and entertaining close friends when they visited, he took up snorkeling and spear fishing off his private beach. Like Rachel Carson, he did not venture far from shore. When I visited Goldeneye in 1985, while working as an oceanographer in Kingston, Jamaica, Fleming's house appeared plain and its landscape overgrown. Fleming seems to have designed his Caribbean premises as an escape from English society and not as a show piece for visiting ex-pats.

Edward Whitehouse and Ian Fleming both served in Britain's wartime navy, they both smoked like chimneys, took a crack at writing, and influenced my view of the sea, but one did not attain the other's publishing success, wealth or fame. Nor did my father suffer a premature death as an unhappy man. In the 1960s, Jamaica was paradise, but Fleming's life was not. By the 1950s, he was already smoking sixty to seventy cigarettes a day, and drinking heavily in the evening hours. He died of heart failure in 1964, when he was fifty-six years old.

At the age of forty-three, within weeks of writing his first Bond novel, the long-time bachelor married a British socialite. They had a child together and bought a London-retreat house in St. Margaret's Bay, England, which is close to Dover. But despite this new found companionship and career, and his subsequent commercial success as an author, Fleming did not achieve desired respect within British society, which the Fleming family name had in spades and his mother sought for him. Nor did he become independently wealthy

---

[104] B.A. Rosenberg and A.H. Stewart, *Ian Fleming* (Boston: Twayne Publishers, 1989), 5.

until the last few years of his life. During the early years of James Bond, the royalties from the U.K. editions of his books were on the order of a few hundred pounds sterling. His first book, which was published in the UK just eleven years before his death, was also swiftly rejected by all three of the big name US publishers he sent it to.

In his youth, Ian Fleming sometimes referred to his mother as 'M', the moniker he also assigned to James Bond's boss. When your grandfather is a self-made millionaire and your father's obituary appears in the London *Times*, written by Winston Churchill, your relatives and peers hold you to very high expectations. But during the early years of James Bond, in the halls of a fading empire, and in the homes of port and sherry, Ian Fleming's older brother was whispered to be the better writer.

In addition to serving in the Royal Navy, both my father and Fleming completed special training in Canada, except in Fleming's case it occurred in Oshawa, which is near Toronto, on the shores of Lake Ontario. It took place during the war at a school for covert (i.e. secret) agents run by the Manitoba-born Canadian Sir William Stephenson, who is sometimes referred to as "the Quiet Canadian", or the man known by the wartime intelligence codename "Intrepid". Stephenson was a real spy, and like Edward Whitehouse he was a man of few words. He is recognized as one of the great secret agents of the twentieth century. Like Fleming's grandfather, he was a self-made millionaire. Like James Bond's famous 'Q', Stephenson was fascinated by gadgets, and like Bond himself he drank martinis. He even helped found America's and Great Britain's secret services, flew fighter planes in World War I, and became a European lightweight amateur boxing champion. "For Fleming, Stephenson was almost everything a hero should be."[105] Sir William and Commander Fleming worked together, to such an extent that Stephenson could

---

[105] Ibid., 123.

also be known as the man who inspired Ian Fleming—but who would believe James Bond was born in Winnipeg? They became life-long friends, but publicly Fleming could not identify spies he knew. He acknowledged the author of the Bulldog Drummond books as the forerunner of Bond, and with certainty James Bond is not one person but an amalgamation of Fleming's personal experiences, desires, and fantasies.[106]

Fleming wrote his first novel, *Casino Royal*, in just twelve weeks. He wrote his second, *Live and Let Die*, in twelve fewer days and it was several thousand words longer. Respect within English society eluded him, but creativity did not. Fleming wrote the first Bond novel in 1952. This occurred one year after Rachel Carson published *The Sea Around Us* in the United States and the same year Jacques Cousteau released *The Silent World* in the UK. The book's plot is partially based on an actual casino experience Fleming had in Lisbon, while enroute to New York in 1941, to meet J. Edgar Hoover and the Quiet Canadian. One of the double-O missions described in *Casino Royal* is based on a secret break-in Sir William Stephenson conducted in New York. Fleming was allowed to tag along. The future Bond author probably also became aware of 'Station M'.[107] Stephenson set it up in Canada during the war as a subversive technology development laboratory, under the cover of the Canadian Broadcasting Corporation, the now famous home of *Hockey Night in Canada*. It became "...the foremost training ground for sabotage and subversion in the New World."[108]

Ian Fleming actually participated in the secret agent training program at Station M. Although the program proved he lacked the characteristics required to kill in cold blood at close range, Fleming scored his highest mark in the underwater training exercise. It

[106] Ibid., 18.
[107] Ibid., 123.
[108] Ibid., 127.

required him to fix a mine to a ship's hull after a long underwater swim, similar to what James Bond accomplished in the movie *Live and Let Die*. When discussing Fleming's time at Oshawa, biographer John Pearson concludes, "The school not only provided him with a lot of tricks which he was to pass on to James Bond, but it helped him to decide, when the time came to decide, just what kind of an agent Bond must be."[109]

Six years after the publication of *Casino Royal*, Fleming's *Dr. No* introduced us to the luscious marine biologist Honey Rider, played by Swiss goddess Ursula Andress in the movie version of the book. The movie was not released until 1962. Like Fleming himself, Rider swam and fished from the beaches of a Caribbean island. Fleming was on the set for the scene, which he arranged to be shot on a Jamaican beach, not far from Goldeneye. If commercial sales are an indication, *Dr. No* and its accompanying movie captivated a generation. John F. Kennedy, who was president of the United States at the time, requested a private viewing of the film at the White House. This movie, and the ones that followed, made Fleming a very famous man, but by then he was too ill to enjoy it. He died two years after staring into the eyes of Ursula Andress on a white-sands beach. Alcohol and cigarettes robbed him of the glory creativity would have brought to a longer life.

Ian Fleming died the same year as Rachel Carson. Both left government jobs to become full-time writers. Both applied their public service experience to their writing. Unlike Fleming and Cousteau, however, Rachel Carson had neither a spouse nor well-connected affluent family to draw upon during her formative years. Rachel Carson and Ian Fleming died in their late fifties, one year before the release of the blockbuster Bond movie *Thunderball*. From the standpoint of influencing the baby boomer's view of the sea, *Thunderball* is Fleming's definitive movie. It includes scuba scenes

---

[109] Ibid., 129.

and underwater equipment that would have been state-of-the-art at the time, such as single hose scuba valves and subsea personal scooters. This is, however, the point where Fleming's direct influence upon our view of the sea becomes murky. *Thunderball*, the book, is based on a movie concept by the same name, not vice versa, and the movie script did not belong to Ian Fleming alone. He and his advisers had their day in court before conceding to an out-of-court settlement with two Americans. The movie was released in 1965, thus I speculate that inclusion of a dazzling collection of fully-functional and state-of-the-art underwater technologies was the work of the movie's producers and production crew.

There is no doubt that it was the Bond movies, and not the books themselves, that influenced my view of the sea. Their effect on me was more a matter of Hollywood. I say this figuratively as famed Bond movie producers Albert Broccoli and Harry Saltzman were based in London, but I also say this unequivocally because I did not read any of the Bond books as an adolescent. Regardless, the movies are based on Bond, who is undeniably Fleming.

Ian Fleming influenced my view of the sea, and like my father and Jacques Cousteau his view was influenced by his country's navy. But Fleming's influence upon me is not independent of the other two. While marketing his first novel in 1953, Ian Fleming attended a party in London sponsored by the publisher Hamish Hamilton. There he first met one of this publisher's newest clients, Jacques Cousteau.[110] They must have hit it off as Cousteau invited Fleming to join him on his latest adventure, the raising of a Greek trading vessel in the Mediterranean. Fleming spent two weeks with Cousteau and his diving team. Cousteau gave him an autographed copy of *The Silent World*, and in the relationship that followed, Cousteau became Fleming's "favorite character".[111] I speculate that

---

[110] Lycett, *Ian Fleming: The Man Behind James Bond*, 241.
[111] Ibid., 264.

this is why Ian Fleming continued to refer to scuba diving as aqualunging, years after the public had abandoned Cousteau's terminology. Fleming is also quoted as saying that he is "aiming to become *the* journalist of the underwater world."[112]

Thus, in the same year Edward Whitehouse quit the Royal Navy, the man with the golden typewriter stood next to the world's greatest underwater explorer. This occurred first in England and then again on the decks of *Calypso* in the Mediterranean. Fleming became a fan of the undersea world of Jacques Cousteau fourteen years before the American public saw the television series by the same name. Parts of the Bond novel *Live and Let Die*, which was published the year after Fleming and Cousteau first met, are based on newspaper articles Fleming wrote about Cousteau's underwater explorations.[113]

Like everyone else, Fleming's view of the sea is an amalgamation of his life experiences, which included Cousteau's view of the sea. By projecting this view onto the movie screens of the western world, Ian Fleming and his associates in the film industry injected seemingly independent confirmation of the scuba sea. Cousteau's aqualung is limited in terms of the depth to which it can be used, but the man's influence upon our view of the sea appears to be fathomless. The adventures of James Bond extended the Cousteau view well beyond the Frenchman's direct reach.

Jacques Cousteau is likely only one of several individuals who influenced Ian Fleming's view of the sea. I can only speculate, because Fleming spent formative years within the secretive world of naval intelligence, but it is said that during World War II, before the United States officially entered it, the American oceanographer Athelstan Spilhaus aided Britain's antisubmarine warfare program by leaking the design of his bathythermograph to them. They also gave it

---

[112] Pearson, *The Life of Ian Fleming*, 244.
[113] Rosenberg and Stewart, *Ian Fleming*, 6.

to the Canadians as it was an essential tool for determining the effectiveness of sonar sensors used for antisubmarine warfare.[114]

The United States and Britain shared other ocean intelligence during the same period.[115] While working via the British Admiralty's Swell Forecasting Section, for example, they pooled meteorology and oceanography expertise to design and establish wave monitoring and forecasting infrastructure for the English Channel, in aid of amphibious operations such as the invasion of Normandy. This involved the work of pioneering oceanographers whose names and discoveries continue to be referenced in oceanographic texts. References do not state explicitly, thus I speculate this information ended up in the Admiralty's hydrographic section, which interacted with Rear-Admiral Godfrey's Special Branch during the war. Thus, it is conceivable that knowledge of this cooperative activity reached the desk of Ian Fleming. This would place Fleming with oceanographic pioneers, and among founding members of the field of ocean intelligence.

---

[114] Mills, "Canadian Marine Science from Before *Titanic* to BIO," 12.
[115] Hamblin, *Oceanographers and the Cold War*, 42.

Chapter Twelve

What I Saw

I respected my father and the navies he served. Both influenced my view of the sea. But Jacques Cousteau and Rachel Carson inspired me, James Bond and a bottle-nose dolphin entertained me, the Bond girls and the driver of a yellow submarine stimulated me, Jaws kindled inner fears, and the coast guard gave me a job. Collectively, these experiences and perceptions provided a view of the sea that drew me to the profession of oceanography.

Like Jacques Cousteau's wife, my mother married a voyaging navy man after a one year courtship via pen, paper and post. In October 1953, my parents emigrated to Canada. My mother was born in October and tells me she received two birthday presents at sea that year–a handbag and me. Born Canadian, I had little sense of my British heritage. During the early years in Canada, Eddy, as my mother called my father, ate kippers for breakfast and sometimes tomatoes fried in bacon fat. I still like beans on toast, cheese on toast, marmalade on toast, and sometimes just butter on toast, and of course roast beef and Yorkshire pudding. Otherwise, with the exception of a few ex-Royal Navy friends of my parents, who also emigrated to Canada in the 1950s, by the time I went to university there were no tell-tale signs of the family's origin. By then, we were all Canadian.

I did not reconnect with my British heritage until after graduate school. I received a post-graduate fellowship to conduct oceanographic research in Germany, and used the opportunity to explore Europe for the first time. Whenever my heart pined for roast beef and Yorkshire pudding, washed down by the finest pint you'll find on earth, my mother's sister and her husband in England took me in, repeatedly.

Auntie Doris lives in the small village of Catworth. It has one lane, bordered by brick and stucco houses, private gardens and farmland. At the top of the lane, a bend in the road and a small garage point the way to the neighboring village of Kimbolton, while a short side lane passes the village church on its way to the farmlands of Little Catworth. With the exception of lorries passing through to Kimbolton and towns beyond, and the odd farm vehicle or horse, you were just as likely to look out of Auntie's window and see someone on foot, as someone driving a car down the narrow lane. During my post-graduate years, the focal point of the lane was the village pub and its adjacent store, which also housed the post office. From there, Uncle Jack fetched his daily papers and Auntie their pension allowance. Their house, like others on the lane, was literally a stone's throw from the pub.

Catworth also provided a base from which to explore England-at-large. During the years that followed I drove the moors, photographed the Cotswolds, explored James Herriot's Lake District, walked with sheep, shared chocolate biscuits with the family dog in a countryside bed and breakfast, and arrived in a fog-consumed village as if I was in an episode of the *Avengers*. My most memorable trips were to Newcastle-Upon-Tyne, to visit my mother's mother, Grandma Taylor. A pensioned widower in her eighties, she smoked throughout the day and sometimes bet on the ponies, with a keen eye. In morning, she would turn on the gas cooker to prepare me a proper British breakfast, in a frying pan that perpetually housed a quarter-inch of congealed bacon fat. But instead of lighting the gas burner, she used the lit match to light a cigarette, while turning to me to chat about something, the gas hissing all the while. In hindsight, I now realize she was messing with me, a rare bit of entertainment for a lonely widow. Once, after I had spent the night drinking with a friend, Grandma displayed the full breadth of her mind-messing breakfast talents by floating a piece of bread in the liquefied bacon grease. Even her cat, Timmy, shied away from it. I always suspected that sometimes cigarette ash dropped into Grandma's breakfast pan, but with the diversity of its contents, I could never prove it.

On Sunday mornings in Catworth, I sometimes felt like a character in a Thomas Hardy novel, as I walked the farm-bordered lane to Little Catworth, and then joined Uncle Jack for a stroll to the village pub for a pre-dinner pint. The pub has changed hands many times since my first visit, but it always retains its name, *The Race Horse*. One of my treasured pleasures in life is sampling pints pulled in this pub, while accompanied by my Uncle Jack. There, I learned that in the countryside a pub's closing hour is just a guideline, like the pirates' code. It is intended for tourists like me, but not when I am with my Uncle Jack. Often, we exited the pub into cool air and light mist of late evening, for the short walk up the lane. I remember Uncle Jack walking with pipe in hand and a click to the heels of his shoes, and me with a buzz on and a privileged sense of belonging. With my aunt already in bed, we would finish the night in their living room, with pork pies from the half-sized fridge, boxes of biscuits, and a dose of British tellie.

Decades after my inaugural visit, the pork pies were on my mind as I stood behind the hearse that carried Uncle Jack's lifeless body. Bespectacled and graying, I joined his son and other family members as we walked from their home to the church just beyond. On the day before, for the first time, I had entered *The Race Horse* without him, for a pint, but the taste was not the same.

In a village like Catworth, everyone you bury is family, regardless of blood. During a funeral, they are all in the church courtyard, either standing by the open grave or lying nearby with tombstones of years and centuries past. Catworth preserves evidence of family and community, for generations, for tradition, for people like me. By then, I too felt like family. England had re-entered the Whitehouse blood.

My father did his best to keep his British heritage from the lives of his children, but without success. I discovered a different England than the one he experienced, as the lure of family and tradition drew me from his view. Through personal experience, not advice, I discovered that the confines of economic and social stature are like going to sea. It is not where you start that defines you. It is what you choose to make of it. Just as my father and I developed different views of England, we developed different views of the sea. Within each of us there is commonality, but there are also personal experiences that shape our overall sense of the sea. Some experiences weigh more than others.

In 1962, a stunning blonde from Sweden, Ursula Andress, waded out of the Caribbean Sea and onto the set of Albert Broccoli's and Harry Saltzman's first James Bond movie, *Dr No*. In the book version, Bond author Ian Fleming names her Honey Rider and Bond finds her nude, collecting sea shells. In the movie version, she is the daughter of a marine biologist who specializes in zoology, and Bond finds her on Dr. No's forbidden white-sand beach wearing a matching 1960s era bikini. Forty-seven years later, when I mentioned this Bond scene during drinks with matching middle-aged men, they recited Ursula's name as if they had just seen her that morning.

One year after Honey Rider branded her view of the sea into the minds of adolescent and adult males, the bottlenose dolphin Flipper hit the big screen in a movie by the same name, which was soon followed by a television series. The theme song for *Flipper* was one of those simple tunes you cannot get out of your head ("They call him Flipper, Flipper..."). The script featured a warden, who worked to preserve the marine life of Florida, and his two sons, who spent their time playing with Flipper. The television series, which ran until 1967, juiced up the male demographics by including a scuba-diving female oceanographer, who came with her own yellow submarine. She was Swedish too.

In 1965, while Flipper and his oceanographer friend were turning us spoony, James Bond's producers released another blockbuster, *Thunderball*. It featured Caribbean-blue seas, state-of-the-art underwater technology, and of course Claudine Auger–Miss France, first runner-up to Miss World, and scantily clad in the latest fashions and scuba gear.

Apparently, the public view at the time was that warm, aqua-blue seas and nearly naked, scuba-diving female biology enthusiasts with foreign accents dominated the marine science scene, when in reality it was dominated by sea-going white men working on classified geophysical projects funded by the US and Soviet navies. From the perspective of stimulating the mind, one vision is fantasy, the other a cold shower.

Within a year of *Thunderball*, however, another foreign accent shattered this view, also French but not contrived to target the sexual fantasies of males. The voice and image of Jacques Cousteau became synonymous with the "seven seas". He became a world-wide phenomenon when he delivered the rewards of the aqualung to our living rooms through his television series, *The Undersea World of Jacques-Yves Cousteau*. Although it has been more than thirty years since I saw an original episode of this television series, I still recall the dramatic opening bars of its theme song.

Television was the primary distraction for kids in our neighborhood in the 1960s. With the exception of the odd popularized series such as *The Hardy Boys* and *Nancy Drew*, kids reading something other than school books were not common where I lived. I was a slow reader and still am. Like my friends and brothers, in the 1960s I was glued to the tube. Eventually, television drew me to the occasional book about the environment, particularly Rachel Carson's books. Like my father's wartime view in the navy, Carson's *Silent Spring* view is not pleasant, but through this book Carson inspired an interest in environmental toxicology.

Television was great, but I also frequented the cinemas of Halifax. In 1975, if you saw the movie *Jaws,* the marine biologist's version of *The Exorcist*, then you probably have a different view of the sea. After watching *Jaws*, a few of my scuba-diving friends started checking under the keel before descending into the dim-light world of marine adventure. To this day, my scuba diving wife refuses to watch it.

If the first version of *Jaws* wasn't enough to color your sea red with blood, maybe its 1978 sequel did it for you, or the next in 1983, or the subsequent one in 1987, or the video-game version that came years thereafter. And if you think the beast is dead, go ahead, scuba dive, but don't watch the 2006 movie, *The Holiday*, particularly the scene in a video rental store. A movie theme song writer played by actor Jack Black tries to impress his female companion (Kate Winslet) by recalling a few of the most famous theme songs of the boomer years. When he sings a line from Simon and Garfunkel's theme song for *The Graduate*, with the movie's lead actor (Dustin Hoffman) standing in the next aisle, you chuckle with fond memory. But when he sings just two notes–"ba dum" in a tenor voice, while holding a rental copy of *Jaws*, he awakens a gremlin of the inner mind.

When I was eleven, with my father's permission I enrolled in naval sea cadets, but when I was twelve my father took a rare deviation from navy life. He gave me a choice. Although his disposable income was negligible, he was willing to fund a summer of activity. I could either spend my time with the sea cadet band at its camp in Cornwallis, Nova Scotia, or I could abandon sea cadets and take sailing lessons through the Royal Canadian Naval Sailing Association, Halifax Squadron. I chose the latter, and with this decision I unknowingly set a new direction for my view of the sea.

I had chosen a seemingly civilian summer, away from the sea cadets, but the sailing club took me closer to the navy than a summer at Cornwallis could ever provide. The Halifax Squadron was located on a naval base, at the mouth of Halifax harbor, where it remains today. Just as Rachel Carson's beloved summers of adulthood were spent on the rocky shores of Maine, my beloved summers of youth were spent on the docks of the yacht clubs of Nova Scotia. Eventually, I decided that in addition to racing dinghies, I wanted to be a sailing instructor, but it required additional qualifications.

In the 1960s and 70s, the Halifax Squadron had its own approach to qualifying its youth. As a means of diversifying my qualifications, I stood for my whalers ticket. A whaler is a twenty-seven foot open boat the navy uses for multiple purposes, one of which is sailing. The examination for my ticket was entirely practical. We left shore on a typical bluenose August morning, with a navy crew and me, and the well full of rum. We spent the night on a beach off Sambro and returned the next day—the crew unshaven and me with a ticket in hand. Forty years later, it remains among my most cherished possessions, signed 29 August 1970 by then Squadron Rear-Commodore Ross Menzie.

In the early to mid-1960s, pride was something the Royal Canadian Navy wore on all decks. After all, when France fell to the Germans during World War II, before the United States entered the war, Canada was Britain's principal ally at sea.[116] Even after the US entered the war, Canada continued to shoulder a North Atlantic weight well above its means at the time.

The nation responded to this grave responsibility with a show of force. By 1943, Canada had almost two hundred warships in service and almost as many again under construction.[117] The Northwest Atlantic became the only World War II theatre of war commanded by a Canadian.

---

[116] M. Milner, *Canada's Navy: The First Century* (Toronto: University of Toronto Press, 1999), 84.
[117] Ibid., 119.

By the time the war ended in 1945, for a brief period Canada had the third largest navy in the world, comprising more than 400 warships and almost 100,000 personnel.[118] It was also on the cutting edge of naval technology. Unlike Jacques Cousteau, Rachel Carson and Ian Fleming, my father did not feature on the pages of *Life* magazine. But his employer did. The cover of the 27 September 1954 issue featured the Royal Canadian Navy, as a result of its pioneering work with hydrofoils. *Life* considered it to be a "revolutionary idea".

Obviously, the overall size of Canada's navy decreased dramatically after the war. Lower-deck moral went with it, but the cause was not simply a matter of size. After the war, senior British-trained officers tried to re-establish His Majesty's culture within the ranks of rising Canadian and French-Canadian patriotism, without success. Canada's navy redefined itself soon thereafter.

By 1958, it was "big, bold and brash"[119], having shed aspects of British influence in the now NATO and United Nations aligned Royal Canadian Navy. The transition was driven by the Communist threat, with Soviet nuclear submarines boldly hiding among Russian fishing trawlers stationed off the Grand Banks of Newfoundland, and the Chinese assisting North Korea's southern expansion.

Canada combined this post-war military strength with political will, such that during this period it was the only nation to serve on every United Nations peacekeeping mission.[120] By1960, Canada's navy reached its peak in post-World War II strength, and in 1965 it took another step towards breaking free of its Royal Navy culture. That year, the nation gave birth to its red maple-leaf flag, the navy changed its name from the Royal Canadian Navy to the

---

[118] Ibid., 156.
[119] Ibid., 199.
[120] J.L. Granatstein, *Who Killed the Canadian Military* (Toronto: Harper Flamingo, 2004), 4–5.

Canadian Navy, and the British White Ensign flew no more from the sterns of the nation's warships.

By then, Canada's navy was on the cutting-edge of anti-submarine warfare activities, and strongly aligned with the US Navy. Perhaps this aspect, the shedding of British ways, more than any other, is the reason why my father walked with a sense of accomplishment when I was a lad. After all, with the possible exception of hydrofoils during the Cold War, the Royal Navy was and remains superior to Canada's in terms of kit. From a war perspective, the British Navy is the most successful navy of all time. Thus, my father's new-found stride could not have been a matter of technology or the winning of wars.

In 1962, my father introduced me to his new adventure as a naval officer, and to Canada's naval pride. He took me onboard the ship he was serving on at the time, HMCS *Bonaventure*, Canada's last aircraft carrier. Originally of the British Modified Majestic Class, the *Bonnie* arrived in Halifax from its Belfast shipyard in the summer of 1957, just three years after my father joined the Royal Canadian Navy. Halifax continued to be her home port until decommissioning in 1970.

Largely used for antisubmarine warfare operations during the Cold War, the carrier was state-of-the-art in this particular aspect and the central component of Canada's then formidable naval power. In 1962 the *Bonnie* was a member of NATO's Western Atlantic fleet during the Cuban missile crisis. The carrier was on NATO exercises at the time, docked in England. When the order to join the fleet came down, the aircraft carrier left port so fast that it left several dozen crew ashore.

For the first time in my life, at the age of eight and with my father by my side, I stood at the entrance to a massive ship. It was small by aircraft carrier standards, but at 700 feet in length and 40 feet just to her landing deck, it appeared humongous in the eyes of a lad. With nine decks plus the tower, you could hear her voice, smell her breath, and feel her power.

Its presence commanded you to such depth that half a century later, I sense her void when I work next to her former Halifax berth, under the Angus L. MacDonald Bridge. For half a century since, nothing has commanded that berth like HMCS *Bonaventure*, at least in my mind. Although the building I frequent is home to Canada's east-coast submarine operations, no one else even mentions the fact that the void in front of them was once home to a world-class aircraft and anti-submarine warfare carrier. This causes me to wonder whether it is the ship itself or the sense of naval pride that I miss. Or perhaps it is the man who walked me up her gangway.

As I stood before the *Bonnie's* gangway on that 1962 day, I understood what it meant to be part of naval culture and tradition. I looked up at my father and saw him as I had not seen him before. Wearing his officer's uniform, which by that time bore several rows of service ribbons and two rings on its cuffs, he looked down at me with a rare grin. We climbed the gangway, with me in front and Lieutenant Whitehouse bringing up the rear. With Canada's naval pride lying in front of him, and me already standing on board, my father stepped onto the deck of HMCS *Bonaventure* as its quartermaster saluted him smartly.

On HMCS *Bonaventure* my father taught me how to use a ship's ladder–always facing backwards, hand over hand, keeping your chest close to the rungs as you descend. Our destination was the bowels of the aircraft carrier. He was going to show me the engine room, his home away from home. With a twenty-six foot draught displacing more than 20,000 tons of water, we had a ways to go. As I descended, on ladder upon ladder and through companionways of no obvious direction, I became disoriented in the presence of increasing heat and noise. Somewhere below the waterline, childhood fears overwhelmed me. As a result, our final destination eluded us that day. Although he never spoke of it, I must have disappointed him.

Regardless of deck or rank, the officers and crew of HMCS *Bonaventure* took pride in getting the job done.

I remember little more of that day on my father's aircraft carrier. Fourteen years later, when we again stood together at the entrance to a massive ship, a weather ship headed for weather station Papa, neither of us recalled this *Bonnie* day. By then, we both knew it was nothing to reminisce about. Given that my father was enrolled in a British naval academy at the age of eleven, I doubt he accepted my eight years of age as an excuse for not making it to the *Bonnie's* engine room in 1962. But this is not the reason why, years later, a once proud Canadian naval officer advised me not to join the navy. He did not blame a lad for his change of heart towards the Canadian Navy. He blamed it on Canada's then minister for National Defence–Paul Hellyer. If you wish to inflict sadness upon a senior Canadian Navy man, just mention this period.

In the mid-1960s, Paul Hellyer developed a plan to integrate Canada's army, navy and air force into a single command structure. The plan was designed to eliminate duplication and improve communication between the three branches of the armed forces. Hellyer left his ministerial position at National Defence in 1967, the same year Parliament passed his *Canadian Forces Reorganization Act.* When it came into effect the following year, the Canadian Navy ceased to exist as such. And to ensure that my father no longer viewed himself as a navy man, the now unified Canadian Forces stripped him and his fellow sailors of their naval uniforms, giving all those who serve–army, navy and air force–a common turf-green suit. Due to its color, it is said, jokingly, that the uniform's cloth was the same used for gas station attendants.[121]

Paul Hellyer was but one of many influential Canadians who believed the Canadian military was in need of a make-over, but while streamlining the nation's defense structure, Canada inadvertently

---

[121] Granatstein, *Who Killed the Canadian Military*, 82.

humiliated centuries of naval tradition. With the stroke of a pen, navy ranks were obliterated by bureaucrats living far from the sea. For a nation washed by three oceans and several seas, the extent of the humiliation was beyond comprehension. The lowest blow was perhaps the decision that all three services would be assigned a common rank structure based on that used by the army.

Protest was futile and dealt with firmly. Hellyer fired Rear-Admiral William Landymore, a former HMCS *Bonaventure* commander and my father's ultimate boss on the east coast, for resisting the plan. Several other senior naval officers were either fired or simply decided to get out.

The humiliation surpassed what seamen wore, the rank they were assigned and systematic cleansing of the most senior ranks, and it continued after Paul Hellyer departed. While on a NATO exercise in 1969, the 1,350 crew members of HMCS *Bonaventure* learned via the CBC radio that their aircraft carrier, which had recently completed a $17 million refit, was to be scrapped as a component of yet another restructuring and cost-reduction plan.

Within a year of this announcement, my parents moved the family to the warmer weather of Esquimalt, British Columbia. Two years later, my father reached the navy's retirement age and quietly left the service, the same year I enrolled in the University of British Columbia. My science career began when his naval career ended.

Between 1955 and 2003, Canada's expenditures on its armed forces dropped from 7.8 to 1.1 percent of GDP.[122] By 2004, its ranking in the provision of United Nations peacekeepers had dropped to thirty-fourth, but that was its low point. Afghanistan and threat of lost Arctic sovereignty have since forced Canada to resupply and re-kit the nation's army, from new uniforms to state-of-the-art guns and tanks. The Canadian Forces has also procured fleets of new aircraft

---

[122] Ibid., 16.

and is kicking the tires of the F-35, the cutting-edge of fifth-generation fighter jets.

The most symbolic change came in the late summer of 2011, when Defence Minister Peter MacKay announced that the Maritime Command component of the Canadian Forces was returning to its previous name of Royal Canadian Navy, the same name it had when my father joined her ranks in the 1950s. Minister MacKay also announced name changes for the army and air force and stated, "Restoring these historic identities is an important way of reconnecting today's men and women in uniform with the proud history and traditions they carry with them as members of the Canadian Forces. A country forgets its past at its own peril." Polls indicate the Canadian public supports the Minister's decision, but some pundits denounced it. Historian Jack Granatstein called it "abject colonialism", and not surprisingly, Paul Hellyer continued to defend his earlier choice to unify the armed forces under one name.[123,124] Hellyer claimed that returning to the original names would be divisive. If their objections are in specific reference to the word *Royal*, then they are probably right. Otherwise, I speculate Canadian service personnel walk a tad taller today as a result of this change.

Ottawa now realizes its error in trying to legislate away distinction and loyalty within the various branches of the armed forces, but its navy has yet to return to its days of pride on all decks. Once lost, you cannot regain culture and loyalty through procurement and press releases. As stated in 2009 by the navy's most senior officer, Vice-Admiral Dean McFadden, Chief of the Maritime Staff:

---

[123] Meagan Fitzpatrick, "Peter MacKay hails 'royal' renaming of military," *CBC Website,* August 16, 2011 (www.cbc.ca).
[124] Prithi Yelaja, "Royal military renaming slammed as colonial throwback," *CBC website,* August 17, 2011 (www.cbc.ca).

"In order to build tomorrow's fleet we will also have to rebuild the navy institution."[125]

With born and bred navy men like my father advising their sons not to join the navy, it is no surprise to me that the Canadian Forces has a difficult time recruiting and retaining qualified seamen to fulfill operational requirements. In addition to a massive reduction in its ranks since my father joined, the Canadian Forces has struggled to muster a state-of-the-art naval fleet. Its second-hand submarines are in perpetual repair, and the nation has not owned an aircraft carrier since HMCS *Bonaventure* was scrapped almost forty years ago. To this day, the same Sea King helicopters that flew as proud and effective new additions to HMCS *Bonaventure* continue to be used as Canada's antisubmarine warfare helicopters.

I respected my father and the navies he served. Both influenced my view of the sea. But Jacques Cousteau and Rachel Carson inspired me, James Bond and a bottle-nose dolphin entertained me, the Bond girls and the driver of a yellow submarine stimulated me, *Jaws* kindled inner fears, and the coast guard gave me a job. Collectively, these experiences and perceptions provided a view of the sea that drew me to the profession of oceanography. I did not become a marine biologist, but I married a rather attractive one with a French-Canadian accent, and yes she was a scuba diver at the time.

Beyond the role played by Rachel Carson, the ocean science community did not affect my view of the sea significantly during my formative days of youth. I do not recall seeing marine scientists profiled in *Time* magazine. Like others around me, primarily I was influenced by television, the movies and personal experiences. After all, why marine biology? If you wanted to be a scientist, why not a rocket scientist associated with the space program, or a biologist in general? If you wanted to focus on the ocean, why not focus on the

---

[125] "Report on Canada's Navy," *Canadian Defence Review* (August 2009).

most relevant aspects of the field at the time? Why didn't people grow up saying they wanted to be a marine geophysicist?

Even for kids growing up in the United States at the time, there was little to draw upon in terms of academic inspiration. The first graduate degree in oceanography was awarded in the United States in 1930, but by 1958, only 13 of the 2,780 PhDs awarded that year pertained to the sea; only 30 million of a five billion dollar national research and development budget was spent on civilian oceanographic research and surveys.[126] Expenditures increased dramatically thereafter, but by 1971, about two thirds of the money the United States spent on oceanographic research, mapping, and exploration, went to the classified world of the US Navy.[127]

Also, the public's perception of oceanography was obscured by the fact that universities of the day often studied the marine environment within its various earth science departments–biology, chemistry, physics, and geology. The graduate oceanography department I attended in Canada, for example, had only been established for seven years as a separate entity when I arrived in 1978. Prior to that, it was housed in the basement of the medical building, as a component of Dalhousie University's biology program.[128] Oceanography shared the floor with the medical students' lockers and the cadavers located in the medical school morgue.

I did not scuba dive during my time at Dalhousie University, but this had nothing to do with the movie *Jaws*. I do not dive, because like my father and Rachel Carson, I have an angst about being under water. Put me on the water but not in it. Although this affected me when I was eight years old, during my introduction to HMCS *Bonaventure*, I was not truly conscious of it until seventeen years after I became an oceanographer.

---

[126] Wenk, *The Politics of the Ocean*, 37, 39.
[127] Ibid., 13
[128] Riley, "Reminiscences of an Oceanographer," 122.

I realized the true breadth of my angst on a crisp, cool morning, at the age of forty-six, while driving my wife to work and children to school in our 1996 Chevy Blazer. We were driving along the shores of the Atlantic Ocean's St. Margaret's Bay. It was a spectacular winter morning, clear blue sky and 2 °C (36 °F). A slow-moving vehicle in front had caused a line of traffic to build behind, and as we entered a passing stretch I took the opportunity to get by.

By the time I realized the front driver could sense what I could not–ice on the road–it was too late. With the manual four-wheel drive not engaged on this gorgeous morning, the rear end spun out. I compensated with the wheel, too much as it turned out. The vehicle left the road and went airborne off an embankment, towards the Atlantic Ocean. As the vehicle plunged, the weight of its engine brought the nose down, and as the front grill hit December seawater, momentum caused the vehicle to flip onto its roof.

The engine stalled and the cabin grew dark as we sank, with the exception of a beam of light from the rear hatch. From shore, it must have looked like a coffin from Detroit.

The four of us, my wife and I in the front, six-year-old son and eight-year-old daughter in the back, were now suspended upside down by our seatbelts. I do not know how much time passed before our son started to whimper, but there was no blood, broken bones, crying, screaming, or panic. In combination with our seatbelts and the vehicle's design, the water had protected us from injury.

Surrounding sea dampened external noise, creating a surreal sense of calm, but with the sea now engulfing us, our lives were in jeopardy. And as water entered the dim-lit cabin, a single thought came into my mind. It was not directed towards my suspended children and wife beside me, collectively the foundation of my life. Nor was it fear of dying. Isaac Newton taught us that for every action, there is an equal and opposite reaction. When my body became trapped under water that day, my lingering aquatic angst came to the surface of my life. A momentary lack of automotive judgment caused me to realize what decades of life had not. But it did not consume me.

All seamen know that in time of peril, training and action can save a ship and its crew. But neither I nor my marine biologist wife had training or experience in underwater evacuation. Regardless, I knew staying where we were was not an option for survival. I released my seatbelt and dropped into a pool of frigid seawater. The cold focused my mind. As I crawled on the vehicle's submerged roof and into the back seat to be with our children, I continued speaking with my wife in near darkness. Like our children, she remained dry, warm, calm, and suspended up-side-down.

We were unharmed, but the collision of vehicle with water had jammed both front doors shut. The electronically-controlled rear window would not open and there was no manual override mechanism. With the only lit window inoperable, and no tool at hand to break it, our escape route eluded us. It was my daughter who calmly observed that the rear-right door could be opened. From the age of four, when she emerged from her bedroom one morning wearing three skirts at once, like a toddler version of Cindy Lauper, I knew she had a mind of her own.

We agreed on a strategy. The family would assemble next to the operable door, in two teams of two. I would then force the door open and hold it until cabin pressure equalized with water. Then, each team would swim to the surface independently. I would exit first with my daughter. My wife, the professional diver, would follow with our youngest, a non-swimmer at the time.

Memories of this family-defining moment are now a permanent component of my view of the sea. Although years have passed since, my mind returns to it repeatedly, to those final seconds in the rear cabin, when my wife was speaking to me in her soft French-Canadian accent, in the darkness of engulfing sea. Her voice filled my mind as I opened the door to our unknown fate, but our escape strategy was not required. Unknown to us, it was low tide and the tall SUV's roof had come to rest on the bottom. I opened the door not to equalizing seas but to two bystanders standing waist-to-chest deep in frigid water. They were attempting to rescue us, but the doors would not open externally. I waded from sea with child in arms, to an assembly of fire trucks, ambulance, police, and spectators. Onshore the paramedic spoke, but I had yet to return to his world and none of us were physically injured. A kind neighbor drove us to the sanctuary of our sea-side home.

I do not dive, to any depth. I tried it once, using my brother's gear, but the sound of my breath passing through the aqualung consumed me, along with a sense of catastrophe. I do not recall what I actually saw that day. Jacques Cousteau also sensed his breathing at depth, but it had an entirely positive effect upon him: "It is a silent jungle, in which the diver's sounds are keenly heard–the soft roar of exhalations, the lisp of incoming air ...."[129]

Jokingly, I blame my angst on Cousteau and the movie *Jaws*, not genetics, one too many capsized sailing dinghies, or some other childhood trauma. I have a consuming fear that one of those beautiful creatures of the deep will emerge quietly from beneath or behind and pull me to its depths, trapping me in an aquatic coffin. Cousteau experienced a similar fear once, but it was because he was on his first night dive, in seemingly total darkness, and not on the surface like me, but at a depth of twenty-five feet.[130] Cousteau responded to his fear not by surfacing, but by turning off his flashlight to acquire a faint but detectable night vision with ambient light. By the time he surfaced, he reported enjoying the experience.

Perhaps this is why I became an oceanographer who specializes in remote sensing. My particular expertise is viewing the ocean from space, as far from the sea's fearful depths as you can get.

---

[129] Jacques Cousteau with F. Dumas, *The Silent World* (New York: Harper and Row, 1953), 243.
[130] Ibid., 263.

In this twenty-first century, observing the sea with remotely controlled sensors is the norm. Contrary to popular perception, very few oceanographers enter or go beneath the water themselves to study the sea. It is not fear that causes this but the realization that by physically letting go of the sensor, we obtain a different view of the sea. This is not Cousteau's view of the sea. It is not what Ursula Andress saw on *Dr. No's* forbidden beach, nor what Rachel Carson saw on the shores of America. It is not what Flipper's mates saw in the warm waters of Florida and it is not what my father saw while sailing the seas. Moving beyond the baby-boomer view of the sea will help you witness the ocean's impact upon your life, not what you perceive it to be but what it actually is. As in the movie *The Matrix*, this becomes a matter of using technology to gain a sense of what lies above, below and around. We have likely exhausted the major gains we can obtain simply by viewing the sea with our eyes. Jacques Cousteau delivered much of the final chapter of that story.

Chapter Thirteen:

Raising the Future View

As long as they have a passion for the sea, the next Rachel Carson or Jacques Cousteau could come from anywhere. Like a newly-minted college boy, who found himself aboard a coast guard ship heading for weather station Papa, one never knows what the future has in store for those who live by the sea.

Decades after Carson, Cousteau, Fleming, and Flipper, seven years after ocean weather station Papa, and months after oceanography graduate school, in a seemingly unrelated act I began writing to a scuba-diving French-Canadian marine biologist while stationed in Germany. I hardly knew her. Yet, like Jacques Cousteau and Simone Melchior, and like my father and mother, we engaged in courtship via pen and paper.

We met in Canada three years previous. I was a graduate student playing a friendly game of shinny ice hockey with fellow students. Our opponents were staff from the Department of Fisheries and Oceans. She played defense for the Department, picking her way across the blue line wearing knitted mittens and figure skates covered in bright-red stockings. After the game, I caught glimpses of her as everyone sat together in the old Gingers pub. Our paths crossed rarely over the next three years, but in an encounter as bizarre as playing ice hockey in red figure skates, we had our first date the night before I moved to Germany. A few days previous, I had mustered the nerve to invite her to the theatre via telephone. Her soft French accent advised she had already seen the play and with mutual awkwardness we hung up. Less embarrassing than 'I'm washing my hair', I thought, but within minutes the phone rang and she suggested dinner for two. Thirty years later her red skates hang in our basement, rarely used since, but never a thought of discarding them. We married in Kings College Chapel six months after I returned from Germany, on the campus where I received my oceanography degree. We exchanged our vows when political support for Québec separatism was in the flood stage of its cycle. My new-found French-Canadian relatives accepted the English addition to their family unconditionally, in warm Québécois style. In recognition of our respective cultures, however, my wife and I decided to embrace both. If a child was born female she would be given a French name, and if male, an English name.

Our only son, Edward, was born four months after my father died, and grandfather Whitehouse was long gone by then. My son met neither. Nor was he present when my mother stood on the stern of a retired navy man's wooden ketch as it drifted on the Strait of Juan de Fuca, less than a nautical mile from the naval and coast guard docks of Esquimalt. There, my mother spread the ashes of her companion for half a century while her five sons and daughter looked on. There, my father's adventures at sea came to an end, two tacks from where mine began.

Love is not the word that comes to mind when I think of the navy, or when I think of my father as a motherless lad in a British naval academy in the 1930s. Yet, I like to think I loved my father and that the feeling was mutual, even though we both followed naval protocol by never showing it. With honesty, I cannot remember hugging him. Perhaps I confuse love with respect and obedience—the heart of the navy.

I named my son after my father, but I deliberately broke the family tradition of giving him the middle name of George, just as my father broke the tradition of going by his middle name of George, and me by mine. Instead, my wife and I named our son Edward Orion, with the constellation Orion being my evening companion at home and sea. It brightened skies when I was a seagoing oceanographer, conducting nighttime bottle casts and net tows off fantails and observation decks. It also greeted me at my front door the night Edward was born. That night, I entered cool, crisp October air at one in the morning to fetch our transport to the maternity hospital. Orion watched over us for years thereafter as we anchored the family sail boat for short overnighters among the numerous islands of St. Margaret's Bay.

Orion also guided our course as my brothers and I and several friends sailed a wooden schooner in strong winds one night, from St. Peter's to Halifax, dodging fishing boats sailing on auto-pilot. We waited until morning to duck into Liscomb Lodge to disembark those too seasick to finish the journey. Hours after Orion had disappeared from view, we dropped one of my brothers off on a derelict pier in search of a telephone to alert awaiting friends in Halifax. He returned just before noon with a story that a man saw him walking the dirt road wearing his drenched sailing gear. He took my brother in and fed him a hearty breakfast while he spoke of sailing days as a crew member aboard Canada's most famous schooner, *Bluenose 1*.

Orion is not an English name, but with it I will always remember what my British father gave me–an amazing view of the sea. I took my son to sea for the first time when he was two years old, aboard our twenty-seven foot sloop. During that season, and several that followed, he sat tethered to the cockpit, encased in a lifejacket. His favorite activity was eating chocolate chip cookies in heavy seas, pinned to leeward by the heeling hull as the cabin top blanketed him from green ones coming over the bow.

I am anxious skippering in such seas, worried that a critical piece of gear will let go at an unfortunate time, as it did the night we sailed a two-masted schooner from St. Peter's to the French Island of St. Pierre. Pitch dark, with the uncommon combination of thick fog and heavy seas, the helm suddenly felt loose. I shone a flashlight upon the sails in search of a rip, but it was not until the light hit the foredeck that I realized we had lost our forestay, one of the wires that hold up the masts. The wire was still there, but the shackle that attached it to the bowsprit was not. By sailing downwind we were able to keep the masts up while we reattached the forestay to the boat, with my brother hanging half out on the darkened bowsprit and me lying flat on the foredeck behind him, feeding him tools and ready to grab his legs should he lose his grip.

When our son Edward reached the age of twelve, I enrolled him in sailing school. It was a mere two-minute drive from our home. A year later I bought him his first sailboat, but his older sister, who had taken the same road to sea two years earlier, became the accomplished sailor. In some respects, our family is following in the footsteps of my father's house. I am not in the navy, I do not have George to haunt me, and the club we sail out of does not belong to the military. But like my father, I enjoy sitting at the meal table, listening to the kids tell of their adventures at sea and ashore.

My father tried to write about his adventures, then suddenly burned everything he wrote. I did not consciously become a writer. I simply decided to chronicle the lives of family in the form of an annual Christmas letter, a few of which capsulate my children's introductions to the sea. The choice of Christmas as the central theme likely stems from life with my parents. Many households undoubtedly spent more money on Christmas, but I doubt many others put more effort into it than my parents. They generated a level of excitement that prevented us kids from sleeping on Christmas Eve, as we slithered past our parent's bedroom door in the middle of the night, our bellies to the floor, commando style, with the living room Christmas tree as our target. Invariably, my younger brother and I started the ritual too early and my father's voice would growl "get back to bed" from the darkness of his bedroom.

I recalled this childhood memory in 2006, as I stood in my driveway among big flakes of snow and white trees. There was not a sound in the neighborhood, except me stacking firewood. So easy to live the season while missing what it is remembered for. According to my annual Christmas letter, the following year my daughter experienced her first season on a sailing team. The local yacht club has international racing credentials and keeps its junior members training or racing six days per week throughout the summer, with a fleet of parental chauffeurs ferrying them about. By July the skin was peeling off her fingers, but she became the first of the next generation of Whitehouses to complete a nationally-recognized dingy race.

That year the entire family also completed a road trip to Québec City to pick up a Trophy 1703 center-console motor boat. Québec is a remarkable city and as I had warned my English-named son not to mention the Plains of Abraham, we were well received. The locals even commented on how good my wife's French was for someone from Nova Scotia.

Serge the salesman was a splendid vendor, despite his Québec English, but it still seemed strange buying a motor boat from a Frenchman and then towing it 1,100 kilometers (684 miles). In the end it was a great family adventure, except for the bit where the boat trailer kissed the front bumper of a Ford van in a gas station parking lot. Fortunately, I barely touched it and the van's driver was very understanding, in both official languages. Basically, he was parked in my way.

My son, Edward, also joined the sailing team that year except he sailed an Opti, which is not as demanding a dinghy as his sister's Byte. The family took the Trophy motor boat out to watch him sail during the annual club sail past. Once ashore, I reminded Edward that although he was on starboard tack and therefore had the right of way, in a race he would also have been disqualified for hitting that port-tack boat, because he made no effort to avoid a collision.

"Dad, I barely touched him." he responded.

"Ed, you T-boned him" I replied.

"Dad, he was in my way".

With a sense of déjà vu, I became very understanding and changed the subject.

The following year his sister garnered attention by winning her sailing class at ARK–Atlantic Regatta Kanada–which is one of the Canadian junior majors. But rather than continue on the sailing circuit, she beached her boat and flew to London, England, to be with my Auntie Doris. For ten days they hung out in Catworth, went to the theatre in London, shopped, punted in Cambridge, and yes more shopping with my cousins and their families.

The Christmas letter of 2010 noted that Edward had spent the summer terrorizing the docks of the cove in his father's formerly pristine fourteen-year-old Zodiac inflatable boat, which had a peppy eight-horse Yamaha engine on the back. When Edward ripped the side out of one pontoon on a neighbor's metal ramp, the event was categorized as a learning experience. But when another neighbor telephoned to complain about a boy in a Zodiac, Edward was served five days without the boat and a lecture on why yet another neighbor called him *Fast Eddie*.

On his first day back at sea, Edward left the dock at half throttle. In search of a parent to witness his nautical transformation, he fixed his view on our house behind him. With its skipper looking aft, the boat ran into yet another neighbor's wharf and then rode up its float like a prop in a Burt Reynolds' movie, with its engine whining out of water. I stood cross-armed and silent at our living room window, feeling much like my father and wondering how many wharves Edward planned on visiting that summer.

Eventually, I realized that my Christmas letters were chronicling our lives as a maritime family. Unlike my father's family, my family encouraged me to write and to share what I had written. Had I not done so, I would not have realized that my children had established deep family roots before they were old enough to vote. Although my daughter's sailing credentials exceeded those of her father when he was her age, she gave up the chance to take the journey to a national racing event. Instead, she chose to visit one half of her family roots, in England. Although short-lived, her days on the docks of the yacht clubs of Nova Scotia gave her the skills of a yachtsman and inspired a passion for the sea. That is all I had hoped for. As long as they have a passion for the sea, the next Rachel Carson or Jacques Cousteau could come from anywhere. Like a newly-minted college boy, who found himself aboard a coast guard ship heading for weather station Papa, one never knows what the future has in store for those who live by the sea.

While living in residence at university, my daughter texts and emails me routinely. Unlike my father during my time as an undergraduate, we have the means and desire to correspond as if we still lived in the same household. On a cold February morning she sent a brief but excited message: "DAD LOOK! IF I GET THIS JOB, WORKING 4 MONTHS, 42 HOURS A WEEK AT THAT PAY, THAT'S OVER 9000$!!!! :) :) :)"

She had received an email from the Canadian Coast Guard, enquiring whether she wished to apply to be a deckhand for the summer, in association with the coast guard's Joint Rescue Coordination Center. I sat dumbfounded as I pondered the email's significance. How can it be, I thought, and as a deckhand. Then, my thoughts returned to the docks of Esquimalt harbor, as my father and I stood at the entrance to a coast guard ship. For the umpteenth time I envisioned that wry grin and unusual eye against chalk-grey skin. Yet again, I sensed the traditions that tie. I do not know whether my daughter will get the job, but if she does, I will drive her to the docks of Halifax harbor on her first day. She won't be boarding a massive ship, but somewhere within the coast guard compound I will wish her "Good luck". And I will hug her.

Epilogue:

The Next Carson or Cousteau

I believe that within our youth there exists an as yet unknown view of the sea. My children, who were born on the tail of the echo boom, may or may not develop such a view, but it is certain that the potential for such a person already exists.

When it comes to influencing our knowledge or perception of the sea, can anyone be a Carson or Cousteau, or even Fleming? Is Harvard University Professor Frederick Hunt correct in his view that it is simply a matter of being in the right field at the right time, with the appropriate amount of smarts of course?

Carson, Cousteau, and Fleming proved you need to experience the sea to influence its reflection, and all three were passionate observers. Then again, millions of people experience the sea and are passionate about what they do, but do not influence our view. Experience and passion are not enough. To influence how we see the sea, you require an original view of it, and you must possess a captivating means to deliver that view to the masses. This is a tall order because previously unknown worlds, such as Cousteau's subsea world, Carson's environmental web of cause and effect, and Fleming's insider view of naval intelligence, are not easy to discover or access.

I do not know what this next view will be, but I sense it will not focus on science or engineering, even though our understanding of the sea will only advance with such knowledge. Rachel Carson presented us with facts of science, but *The Sea Around Us* and Silent *Spring* are not science classes. With the application of her poetic writing style, they strike an emotional response. They pluck our fears, awaken our wonder and engage our instinct for survival. Like Jacques Cousteau's *The Silent World*, Carson's books remind us of how wonderful life can be, and if we are not careful our children will not experience that pleasure. Jacques Cousteau did not feed us facts, but he also struck an emotional response. Like Ian Fleming's James Bond and Honey Rider characters, Cousteau presented adventure, stimulated the hormones, and inspired us to travel beyond the mundane of daily ritual. Fleming interwove fact and fantasy to such great success that at times even experts had difficulty distinguishing between the two.

Rachel Carson also proved you do not need to be in the navy to appreciate the sea or change the way people view it. She did, however, encapsulate the scientific discoveries of war. Major advances in our understanding of the sea and its boundaries are linked to national security, and nothing influences the state of the sea like wind and war. Influential wars, however, are episodic and as observed by Frederick Hunt, major advancements in a given field are subject to the state of that field. In Hunt's view, the focus is not on the gifted individual but upon their positioning and how they choose to apply what lays before them. Hunt's view is the socialist view. Anyone can be famous.

Individuals who started from the elite positions of wealth and well-connected families influenced our view of the sea, but it has also been influenced by others. Their common factor is not money. In addition to having an original view of the sea and a means to deliver it to the masses, they alter perception through novel application of emerging knowledge. They obtained their novel view of the sea by acquiring knowledge largely unknown by the public. Focusing entirely on underlying technology or the funding required to create it will not result in a new view of the sea. The French engineer Émile Gagnan, for example, co-invented the aqualung, but he is not credited with changing our view of the subsea.

As the biographer Madsen observed in his closing chapter on Cousteau, the man was not a scientist, but he was what the science community needed most. Presumably, Madsen refers to Cousteau's ability to influence our view, and the fact that scientific research requires public funding, which is governed by perception, not by science. This is also common to Rachel Carson. She wrote about marine science but she did not work as a scientist, even though she held a master's degree in zoology. She proved that someone with scientific training can inspire the masses, but not by sticking to the knitting. The academic career of a scientist advances through publishing in peer-reviewed science journals, which Carson did not do. From the confinements of her 1950s world, Carson was a renegade of science. Just as Cousteau stepped outside of his inaugural profession, the navy, Carson stepped outside of hers. They both proved the value of my father's advice–that a change is as good as a vacation. Except in their cases, by changing professions, they changed the views of an entire generation and beyond.

Then again, the word "change" knows many modifiers. Environmental change, as opposed to professional change, is just as relevant to the quest for a new view. Influences of climate change and the resulting race for sovereignty over the Arctic and Antarctic, for example, will undoubtedly change our view of the sea. They could also result in war. This race has yet to become a military competition, but I speculate the poles of planet Earth are now maggoty with nuclear attack submarines. Obviously, this is a personal view and no single view is ever complete. This is why the individual view always contains an element of subjective perception, no matter how learned it may be. I, for example, live on the shores of one of the Atlantic Ocean's countless indentations. In addition to mine, I can think of five other houses, most within shouting distance, the views from which would lead you to believe you are on the shores of six different coves. Each view is unique even though the space between is but tens to a few hundred meters. Although I have looked out my front window for the past eighteen years, my particular view is never exactly the same, and neither is that of the other five residents. When the weather changes, so does the sky, the surface of the sea, the activities of the people who sail it, and the plants and animals that live there. Extreme weather may also change the cove's coastline for years, if not permanently.

Each resident of the cove could produce an account of the sea, based on their personal view. Each account would be accurate, but incomplete. Even if all six residents combined their views into one, based on years of observation, the result would still be incomplete because they are only looking at the surface of the sea. Also, even over periods of years, they cannot see changes that occur on climatological time scales.

Regardless, the more views you have, the more comprehensive you become and the greater the likelihood of acquiring a novel view. Cousteau once summed up his diving adventures as an attempt to "find the entrance to the great hydrosphere..." Achieving this goal involved more than scuba diving. In his Cousteau biography, Madsen states that when picking new crew for his ship *Calypso*, Cousteau chose people who had more than one skill. One of them could be diving, but diving alone was not enough. Such was the case for Cousteau himself. He was a diver, but he was also a marine cinematographer and a master of public relations.

Similarly, Rachel Carson was trained in the sciences but she was a skilled writer and an experienced public servant. As observed by biographer Linda Lear, Carson realized the time she spent in science graduate school was merely getting something to write about.[131] Also, the time she spent working for the civil service generated strategic contacts and taught her how the political and civil

---

[131] Lear, *Rachel Carson: Witness for Nature*, 80.

systems worked, which proved to be instrumental in her defense and promotion of *Silent Spring*.

The same can be said for Ian Fleming, the creator of James Bond. The time he spent in the intelligence branch of the civil service, and as a journalist covering a Russian spy story, gave him the material and contacts required to create the adventures of James Bond. This included rare contacts within Allied intelligence services, particularly those of the United Kingdom and United States.

This is a fundamental difference between my seagoing father and these three beacons of the sea. Rachel Carson, Jacques Cousteau and Ian Fleming cannot be categorized into a single profession. By wearing several careers, they developed unique views of the sea that drew on all of their previous experiences.

Unfortunately, the descriptive view of the sea provided by Cousteau, Carson and others is no longer in vogue. A modern-day Jacques Cousteau, Rachel Carson or fictional Honey Rider would have difficulty finding a job in the marine sector, despite their expertise in marine biology. This has been the situation for many years and on no occasion have I heard my now teenaged children say they want to become a marine biologist, a Jacques Cousteau, or a Rachel Carson, and certainly not a Honey Rider. During her high school years, only one of my daughter's numerous friends, an intelligent lass from Liverpool, expressed an interest in the profession to me. When they left high school, most went into exotic aspects of engineering, such as biomechanical engineering, or into business school or health sciences, such as the emerging psychological field of neuroscience. My son is taking oceanography in high school next fall, but only because he let his father choose his elective.

My children and their friends love life on the shores of the sea, despite its isolation, and they display genuine interest towards marine wildlife, processes, and phenomena. But colleagues within the marine science community often express difficulty in finding suitably qualified graduate students. Although the US Navy caused a renaissance in oceanographic development in the 1980s, baby boomers raised their children largely unaware of this knowledge. In most cases, they themselves were, and remain, unaware of it.

Sadly, the public's love-in with the biology of the sea, which began and grew during the formative years of the baby boomers, appears to have lost its mojo. I have not researched the subject from a statistical perspective, but if Canada reflects what happened elsewhere, about the time of Rachel Carson's environmental awakening, James Bond's inaugurating marine adventures, and the actions of Presidents Kennedy and Johnson, and about the time of Jacques Cousteau's and Flipper's television series, there was a surge in Canadian involvement in oceanography. I suspect these events are related, even though none of these individuals or characters is Canadian. The surge came later in Canada than in the United States, perhaps influenced by the delay in the development of dynamic oceanography in Canada. In the United States, the 50s and 60s were the heyday of oceanography, with the 70s being a turning point. American field expeditions with oceanographic ships declined in the 1970s as unmanned platforms grew in popularity. The President's Science Advisory Committee and Marine Sciences Council were disbanded during this period, thereby eliminating a strategic and high-level means of liaison for marine scientists. Canada, on the other hand, did not open its now highly regarded Bedford Institute of Oceanography until 1962. Its flagship research vessel, CCGS *Hudson,* completed its most famous cruise in 1970.

The Cold War historian Jacob Hamblin observed a shift away from science during this period towards environmental consciousness. I interpret his observation as the rise of the American environmental movement. Hamblin attributes it to events such as publicized large-scale oil spills, but I sense books such as *Silent Spring* and their political fallout had a broader effect upon the general public. Although descriptive earth science is no longer in vogue, it holds greater public appeal than today's scientific network of environmental monitoring stations and mathematical forecasting models. Math is logical, but it is not the intuitive view of life.

It is not essential that the next beacon of the sea present a descriptive view, but he or she requires the means to reach and subsequently generate an emotional response from the public, whether it be via television, film, theatre, the Internet, cell phone, melodic note or printed word. Thus, by descriptive view I do not necessarily mean just the written word. Although Cousteau's book, *The Silent World*, sold millions of copies, undoubtedly it was his films and television episodes that are responsible for much of the perception he created. Like Rachel Carson, Cousteau was a successful author, but unlike Carson his media of preference was film. Prior to Cousteau, we viewed the sea in two dimensions, even though at the time we knew it had depth. People were always on the sea, never really in it. Not due to fear, like me, but to a lack of means to access it. Émile Gagnan, Philippe Tailliez, Frédéric Dumas, Simon Melchior, and Jacques Cousteau were all on the vanguard of technologies that ultimately led to the world of scuba diving. Cousteau stands out because he approached the aqualung as a descriptive view to an unknown world.

In my heart, the opportunity to change public perception of the sea still exists, and there are analogies in other professions. Are the popular television programs *American Idol* and *So You Think You Can Dance* influencing student applications to artistic schools and colleges, and to public and private funding of such institutions? I particularly enjoy segments when the judges and Emcees debate whether the respective show is a singing or dancing competition or a popularity contest. It is a matter of perception.

This suggests that although my daughter and her friends are studying fields seemingly far removed from the sea, they could still become a Carson, Cousteau or Fleming. I, for example, did not think of the coast guard when I was studying quantum mechanics. Thus, I believe that within our youth there exists an as yet unknown view of the sea. My children, who were born on the tail of the echo boom, may or may not develop such a view, but it is certain that the potential for such a person already exists.

Recently, I had a conversation with a young surgeon. Uncharacteristically, the surgeon started telling me about his life, in addition to me telling him about mine. He said that if he was to do it all over again he would become a lobster fisherman or oceanographer. Some would consider such a move to be a serious error in judgment, but not me. After all, the renowned Norwegian oceanographer Bjorn Helland-Hansen studied medicine before turning his attention to marine science.[132]

It had been years since I had heard someone refer to marine science as "cool" and it took me by surprise. I was looking into the eyes of a man in his late twenties to early thirties, who in addition to being exceedingly well educated had achieved my parents' definition of ultimate professional success. Yet his heart belonged to the sea, where the mundane rituals of examining the prostate and colon of middle-aged men are washed away. This lure of the sea has existed for generations and apparently it is alive today, awaiting the means to inspire yet another generation.

He held this view even though he came well after the heyday of marine biology and oceanography. Although he discovered I was an oceanographer, the surgeon did not ask whether I scuba dive. Cousteau's final sentence in *The Silent World* states that the future conquerors of the deep will need to get wet. If by this he means they will need to experience it first hand, I agree entirely. But if by this he means they will need to scuba dive, I beg to differ.

The surgeon's view was a welcome yet challenging change of course, like bearing away to a spinnaker set when sailing, after a long

---

[132] E.L. Mills, *The Fluid Envelope of Our Planet: How the Study of Ocean Currents Became a Science* (Toronto: University of Toronto Press, 2009), 106.

and wet beat to windward. Here, at last, was the potential for a new view of the sea. After all, "...human health is inextricably linked to ocean health, and vice versa."[133] Or as summarized by William Fenical: "Comprising 34 of the 36 Phyla of life, marine ecosystems are indeed our last genetic diversity and biotechnological frontier; terrestrial systems possess only 17 Phyla. We have much to learn."[134] Bacteria growing among the coral keys of Florida, for example, produce a chemical called largazole, which medical researchers believe holds promise for the treatment of bone diseases and fractures. Yet, human activity is decimating the planet's coral reefs, perhaps irrevocably. Even if you live thousands of miles from a reef, you are part of the problem because elevated atmospheric temperatures, resulting from influences of greenhouse gases, are responsible for episodically bleaching the life out of coral reefs.

This brings us back to the argument that the future view is about finding the next gifted individual. This is the *ninety percent of science accomplished by ten percent of scientists* approach. It suggests that even if you subscribe to Frederick Hunt's percolator hypothesis, you still need educated individuals to move a field forward.

Currently, the vanguard of oceanography is following the path of meteorology, but the gap between is narrowing. Although both environments hold mystery, the ocean is still perceived as being a frontier. The greater the unknown, the greater our fears, the greater the untapped adventure, and the greater the likelihood of plucking the perceptions of the public view. My oceanographic sensors and platforms view of the sea recognizes the benefits of forecasting

---

[133] L.E. Fleming and E. Laws (eds.), "Special Issue on the Oceans and Human Health," Oceanography: *The Official Magazine of the Oceanography Society* (June 2006), 18.

[134] W. Fenical, "Marine Pharmaceuticals: Past, Present, and Future," *Oceanography: The Official Magazine of the Oceanography Society* (June 2006), 111.

marine environmental change, but to date such benefits have largely been limited to and recognized by academics and mariners. To the billions of landlubbers who live the coastal life, such knowledge is of minor consequence until proven otherwise.

Such will come, and in the meantime I ponder the fact that nine years after Jacques Cousteau published *The Silent World*, Rachel Carson published *Silent Spring*. One silence describes paradise, the other Armageddon–the classic and never-ending case of good versus evil. Neither extreme exists today, and I do not know whether either will be in our future, but with certainty, we now have the means to observe their progress in four dimensions.

Although my profession helped me appreciate the silences of Cousteau and Carson, I still struggle with the silence of my father. He resigned from the Royal Navy three years before Cousteau resigned from the French Navy, and a few years after Ian Fleming left Britain's reserve navy. Having quit the navy and made the formidable decision to change homelands, I still wonder what would be, if after emigrating to Canada he had followed his own advice instead of rejoining the navy. As Doris Day would sing it three years after he emigrated–*Que Sera Sera* (*What will be will be*). Perhaps he thought changing from an enlisted man to an officer was all the change he needed. Perhaps it was. Perhaps he was not trying to influence anyone's view, except his own. I'll never know and I regret not encouraging him to write. Even a scratchy hand-written journal would be priceless to me now. But then, I do not recall any of us kids having the nerve to give him advice.

I wrestle with my father's silence but I did not join the navy, thus I have no problem expressing my opinion on the subject. He gave me that. My father did not write his book, but his advice gave me parts of this one. He gave me one of my views of the sea. The one that goes with me everywhere. The one that is in my blood and causes restlessness when I am away from the sea for extended periods of time. I visit Catworth when I visit England, but I could not live there.

It is too far from the sea. With the exception of a few months here and there, I have never lived more than an hour's drive from someone's navy. When my father advised me not to join the navy, I sense that was his point. It is not the sea itself he steered me from. How can anyone conceived at sea not be drawn to it?

What neither of us realized in 1976, on that day in Esquimalt, as we stood before the gangway to a weather ship designed for meteorology and oceanography, is that I was about to discover the field of oceanography, and that by then the US Navy had become "oceanography's greatest patron."[135] This is why I now subscribe to Frederick Hunt's view that it is a matter of being in the right place at the right time. I continue to recall my father's eyes on that day. I see the slight grin on his face as he looked at me sideways during those final seconds. I see his eyes. They continue to evoke the sense of tradition I felt during that brief but common view of the sea. It was not a naval vessel, and he could not have known then that although he steered me away from the navy, he had just walked me to the navy's greatest contribution to civilian society, next to freedom itself.

---

[135] Hamblin, *Oceanographers and the Cold War*, 32.

Bibliography

Ackleson, S.G. "Light in Shallow Waters: A Brief Research Review." *Limnology and Oceanography* 48, no. 1 (2003): 323-328.

Adams, D. *The Hitchhiker's Guide to the Galaxy.* London: Pan Books, 1979.

Alley, R.B., J. Marotzke, W.D. Nordhaus, J.T. Overpeck, D.M. Peteet, R.A. Pielke Jr., R.T. Pierrehumbert, P.B. Rhines, T.F. Stocker, L.D. Talley, and J.M. Wallace. "Abrupt Climate Change." *Science* 299 (2003): 2,005-2,010.

Ballantyne, I. *H.M.S. London: Warships of the Royal Navy.* Barnsley: Leo Cooper, 2003.

BBC News. "WHO Backs DDT for Malaria Control?" September 15, 2006. http://news.bbc.co.uk/2/hi/science/nature/5350068.stm.

Berenbaum, M. "If Malaria's the Problem, DDT's Not the Only Answer." *Washington Post,* June 5, 2005.

Berque, J., and D. Travin. "Coast-Map-10: A Hydrographic-Based Contribution to Tsunami Preparedness in the Indian Ocean." *Hydro International* (September 2009).

Bevand, P. "Jim Taylor: Wartime Service in H.M.S. *Hood,*" *BBC News.* January 4, 2006. http.//www.bbc.co.uk/ww2peopleswar/ stories/72/a8243372.shtml.

Bissett, W.P., R.A. Arnone, C.O. Davis, T.D. Dickey, D. Dye, D.D.R. Kohler, and R.W. Gould Jr. "From Meters to Kilometers: A Look at Ocean-Color Scales of Variability, Spatial Coherence, and the Need for Fine-Scale Remote Sensing in Coastal Ocean Optics." *Oceanography: The Official Magazine of the Oceanography Society* (June 2004).

Bramwell, M., ed. *The Rand McNally Atlas of the Oceans.* Chicago: Rand McNally, 1977.

Brinton, T. "U.S. Loosens Restrictions on Commercial Radar Satellites." *Space News International (VA)* (October 12, 2009).

Brown, P.J. "US Satellites Shadow China's Submarines." *Asia Times,* May 13, 2010. http://www.atimes.com/atimes/China/LE13Ad01. html.

Burke, L., K. Reytar, M. Spalding, and A. Perry. *Reefs at Risk Revisited*. Washington DC: World Resources Institute, 2011.

Canada's National Programme of Action for the Protection of the Marine Environment from Land-Based Activities (NPA). Government of Canada (June 2000). http://www.ec.gc.ca/Publications/default.asp?lang=En&xml=079B8501-BD2D-43E3-97AF-94E840A140E8.

Canadian Defence Review. "Report on Canada's Navy." (August 2009).

Canadian Environmental Law Association. "Hudson, Quebec Pesticide By-law: Collection of Materials Related to the Supreme Court of Canada Decision on Municipal Powers to Set By-laws." (2003). http://www.cela.ca/collections/celacourts/hudson-quebec-pesticide-law.

—. "Victory for Pesticide Reduction and Local Democracy." (June 28, 2001). http://www.cela.ca/newsevents/media-release/victory-pesticide-reduction-and-local-democracy.

Carson, R. *The Edge of the Sea*. Boston: Houghton Mifflin, 1955.

—. "Life at the Edge of the Sea." *Life,* April 14, 1952.

—. *The Sea Around Us*. New York: Oxford University Press, 1951.

—. *Silent Spring*. Boston: Houghton Mifflin, 1962.

—. *Under the Sea-Wind: A Naturalist's Picture of Ocean Life*. New York: Simon & Schuster, 1941.

—. "Underwater Explorers." *New York Times,* May 13, 1956.

Cleveland, J.S., ed. "Coastal Ocean Optics and Dynamics." *Oceanography: The Official Magazine of the Oceanography Society* (June 2004).

Corson, M.R. "A New View of Coastal Oceans from the Space Station." *EOS: Transactions of the American Geophysical Union* 92, no. 19 (2011): 161-162.

Cousteau, J.Y., with J. Dugan. *The Living Sea*. New York: Harper & Row, 1963.

—, with F. Dumas. *The Silent World*. New York: Harper & Row, 1953.

Crowther, B. "The Real Things." *New York Times,* September 30, 1956.

Curtin, T.B. "Autonomous Oceanographic Sampling Networks: Status Report Through FY 97/Q1." In *Rapid Environmental Assessment: Proceedings of Conference on Rapid Environmental Assessment,* eds. E. Pouliquen, A.D. Kirwan Jr., and R.T. Pearson. La Specia (Italy): NATO SACLANT Undersea Research Center, 1997: 153-164.

Dempsey, D. "Books of the Times." *New York Times,* July 2, 1951.

Dickey, T. "Studies of Coastal Ocean Dynamics and Processes Using Emerging Optical Technologies." *Oceanography: The Official Magazine of the Oceanography Society* (June 2004).

Durgin, C. "Overnight Miss Carson Has Become Famous." *Boston Daily Globe,* July 20, 1951.

Earle, S.A., and L.K. Glover. *Ocean: An Illustrated Atlas.* Washington DC: National Geographic Society, 2009.

ePublic Relations Ltd. "One Small Town Destroys Major Portion of a National Pesticide Market: Seven Lessons for PR, Marketing and Branding Folks." (2001) http://www.epublicrelations.ca/.

Farran, S., and T. Keller. "Students Grade Their Universities." *Maclean's,* February 16, 2009.

Fenical, W. "Marine Pharmaceuticals: Past, Present, and Future." *Oceanography: The Official Magazine of the Oceanography Society* (June 2006).

Fitzpatrick, M. "Peter MacKay hails 'royal' renaming of military," *CBC Website,* August 16, 2011 (www.cbc.ca).

Fleming, I. *Dr No.* London: Jonathan Cape, 1957.

–. *Thunderball.* London: Jonathan Cape, 1961.

Fleming, L.E., and E. Laws, eds. "Special Issue on the Oceans and Human Health." *Oceanography: The Official Magazine of the Oceanography Society* (June 2006).

Fogarty, C.T., R.J. Greatbatch, and H. Ritchie. "The Role of Anomalously Warm Sea Surface Temperatures on the Intensity of Hurricane Juan (2003) During its Approach to Nova Scotia." *Monthly Weather Review* 134 (2006): 1484-1504.

Freuchen, P. *Book of the Seven Seas.* New York: Julian Messner, 1957.

Gosselin, D. "Hellyer's Ghosts: Unification of the Canadian Forces is 40 Years Old, Part One." *Canadian Military Journal* 9, no. 2 (2009): 6-15.

—. "Hellyer's Ghosts: Unification of the Canadian Forces is 40 Years Old, Part Two." *Canadian Military Journal* 9, no. 3 (2009): 6-15.

Gotz, T., G. Hastie, L.T. Hatch, O. Raustein, B.L. Southall, M. Tasker, and F. Thomsen. *Overview of the Impacts of Anthropogenic Underwater Sound in the Marine Environment.* London: OSPAR Commission, 2009.

Granatstein, J.L. *Who Killed the Canadian Military?* Toronto: Harper Flamingo, 2004.

Gue, L. "Why Nova Scotia Should Ban Lawn and Garden Pesticides." *Halifax (NS) Chronicle Herald,* June 20, 2009.

Hamblin, J.D. *Oceanographers and the Cold War.* Seattle: University of Washington Press, 2005.

Han, G. "Interannual Sea-Level Variations in the Scotia-Maine Region in the 1990s." *Canadian Journal Remote Sensing* 28, no. 4 (2002): 581-587.

—, C.L. Tang, and P.C. Smith. "Annual Variations of Sea Surface Elevations and Currents Over the Scotian Shelf and Slope." *Journal of Physical Oceanography* 32 (2001):1794-1810.

Hill, M.N., ed. *The Sea: Ideas and Observations on Progress in the Study of the Seas.* 3 vols. London: John Wiley & Sons, 1962-1963.

HMS *Pembroke*, Royal Naval Barracks, Chatham. *Kent History Forum* (2008). http://www.kenthistoryforum.co.uk/index.php?topic=358.0.

Hunt, F.V. *Electroacoustics: The Analysis of Transduction, and its Historical Background.* New York: John Wiley & Sons, 1954.

Jackson, C.R. *An Atlas of Internal Solitary-like Waves and their Properties.* Alexandria (VA): Global Ocean Associates, 2004.

James Bond Collection: Behind-the-Scenes with Goldfinger and Thunderball. VHS Tape. Los Angeles: MGM/UA Home Entertainment, 1995.

Klamper, A. "Japan's HTV Delivered U.S. Navy Experiments to Station." *Space News International (VA),* September 28, 2009.

Kramer, H.J. *Observation of the Earth and its Environment: Survey of Missions and Sensors, 4th Edition.* Berlin: Springer, 2002.

Lavoie, J. "Salish Sea Looms on Horizon as New Name for Waterways." *Victoria (BC) Times Colonist,* November 4, 2009.

Lear, L., ed. *Lost Woods: The Discovered Writing of Rachel Carson.* Boston: Beacon Press, 1998.

–. *Rachel Carson: Witness for Nature.* New York: Henry Holt, 1997.

– and T. Woodham. "Rachel Carson: Environmental Champion." *Veranda* (April 2009).

Lee, Z.P, C. Hu, B. Casey, S. Shang, H. Dierssen, and R. Arnone. "Global Shallow-Water Bathymetry from Satellite Ocean Color Data." *EOS: Transactions of the American Geophysical Union* 91, no. 46 (2010): 429-430.

Leonard, J.N. "And His Wonders in the Deep: A Scientist Draws an Intimate Portrait of the Winding Sea and its Churning Life." *New York Times,* July 1, 1951.

Life. "Photographic Essay: Underwater Wonders." November 27, 1950.

Louis, G., M-F Lequentrec-Lalancette, J-Y Royer, D. Rouxel, L. Geli, M. Maia, and M. Faillot. "Ocean Gravity Models from Future Satellite Missions." *EOS: Transactions of the American Geophysical Union* 91, no. 3 (2010): 21-22.

Lovejoy, C.E. "Device Aids Underwater Sport." *New York Times,* August 23, 1957.

Lycett, A. *Ian Fleming: The Man Behind James Bond.* Atlanta: Turner, 1995.

Madsen, A. *Cousteau: An Unauthorized Biography.* New York: Beaufort Books, 1986.

Matsen, B. *Jacques Cousteau: The Sea King.* New York: Pantheon Books, 2009.

McKinley, G.A., Fay, A.R., Takahashi, T., and Metzl, N. "Convergence of Atmospheric and North Atlantic Carbon Dioxide Trends On Multidecadal Timescale." *Nature Geoscience Letters,* DOI: 10.1038/NGEO1193 (2011).

McLachlan, D. *Room 39: A Study in Naval Intelligence.* New York: Atheneum, 1968.

Miller, S.D., S.H.D. Haddock, C.D. Elvidge, and T.F. Lee. "Detection of a Bioluminescent Milky Sea from Space." *Proceedings of the National Academy of Sciences* 102 (2005): 14,181-14,184.

Mills, E.L. "Canadian Marine Science from Before *Titanic* to BIO." In *Voyage of Discovery: Fifty Years of Marine Research at Canada's Bedford Institute of Oceanography*, ed. M. Latremouille, (in preparation), 2012.

–. *The Fluid Envelope of our Planet: How the Study of Ocean Currents Became a Science.* Toronto: University of Toronto Press, 2009.

Milner, M. *Canada's Navy: The First Century.* Toronto: University of Toronto Press, 1999.

Mitchell, B.G. "Coastal Zone Color Scanner Retrospective." *Journal of Geophysical Research* 99, no. C4 (1994): 7291-7292.

Morel, A., ed. *Minimum Requirements for an Operational Ocean-Colour Sensor for the Open Ocean.* Reports of the International Ocean-Colour Coordinating Group, no. 1. Dartmouth (NS): IOCCG, 1998.

Munk, W. "The Evolution of Physical Oceanography in the Last Hundred Years." *Oceanography: The Official Magazine of the Oceanography Society* (March 2002).

–. "On the Wind-Driven Ocean Circulation." *Journal of Meteorology* 7 (1950): 79-93.

– and D. Day. "Glimpses of Oceanography in the Postwar Period." *Oceanography: The Official Magazine of the Oceanography Society* (September 2008).

–. "Harald U. Sverdrup and the War Years." *Oceanography: The Official Magazine of the Oceanography Society* (December 2002).

Munson, R. *Cousteau: The Captain and His World.* New York: William Morrow, 1989.

National Geographic Atlas of the World, Eighth Edition. Washington DC: National Geographic Society, 2005.

–: *Sixth Edition.* Washington DC: National Geographic Society, 1990.

National Post (Canada). "U.S. Sub May Have Toured Canadian Arctic Zone." December 19, 2005.

NATO SACLANT Undersea Research Center. *Rapid Environmental Assessment Warfare Support: EXTAC 777 (NATO–unclassified)*. La Spezia (Italy), 2001.

New York Times. "Perspectives for Oceanography." January 18, 1969.

Parker, G. "Wolfville Takes Aim at Lawn Pesticides." *Halifax (NS) Chronicle Herald,* June 8, 2009.

Pearson, J. *The Life of Ian Fleming*. London: Companion Book Club, 1966.

Pouliquen, E., A.D. Kirwan Jr., and R.T. Pearson, eds. *Rapid Environmental Assessment: Proceedings of Conference on Rapid Environmental Assessment.* La Spezia (Italy): NATO SACLANT Undersea Research Center, 1997.

Proc, J. *Radio Communications and Signal Intelligence in the Canadian Navy–Weather Ships*. 2011. http://jproc.ca/rrp/index.html.

Reader's Digest Great World Atlas. Montreal: Reader's Digest Association (Canada), 1984.

Reif, R. "Skin Divers Take Plunge into Blue Paraphernalia." *New York Times,* June 20, 1958.

Renaud, P. "Oceanographic Information Superiority Through Battlespace Characterization." *Sea Technology* (December 2003).

Riley, G.A. "Reminiscences of an Oceanographer." Unpublished manuscript, Department of Oceanography, Dalhousie University (NS), 1984.

Robinson, I.S. *Measuring the Oceans from Space: The Principles and Methods of Satellite Oceanography*. Chichester: Springer-Praxis, 2004.

Rosenberg, B.A. and A.H. Stewart. *Ian Fleming*. Boston: Twayne Publishers, 1989.

Sathyendranath, S., ed. *Remote Sensing of Ocean Colour in Coastal, and Other Optically-Complex Waters*. Reports of the International Ocean-Colour Coordinating Group, no. 3. Dartmouth (NS): IOCCG, 2000.

Schmeck, H.M. Jr. "Ocean Research Urged in Study." *New York Times,* January 12, 1969.

Schmitt, R.W. "Salinity and the Global Water Cycle." *Oceanography: The Official Magazine of the Oceanography Society* (March 2008).

– and E. Montgomery. "Salinity: A Missing Piece in the Climate Puzzle." *Backscatter: The Official Magazine of the Alliance for Marine Remote Sensing Association* (Summer 2000).

Schofield, O., R.A. Arnone, W.P. Bissett, T.D. Dickey, C.O. Davis, Z. Finkel, M. Oliver, and M.A. Moline. "Watercolors in the Coastal Zone." *Oceanography: The Official Magazine of the Oceanography Society* (June 2004).

Sea Technology. "Coral Reef Algae Could Provide Drugs for Bone Diseases." (March 2011).

Sherman, C.H., and J.L. Butler. *Transducers and Arrays for Underwater Sound*. New York: Springer, 2007.

Showstack, R. "Obama Administration Announces Ocean Policy." *EOS: Transactions of the American Geophysical Union* 91, no. 31 (2010): 271.

Smith, E.H. "A Practical Method for Determining Ocean Currents." *Bulletin of the United States Coast Guard* 14 (1926): 50pp.

Snowie, J.A. *The Bonnie: HMCS Bonaventure*. Erin, ON: Boston Mills Press, 1987.

Stommel, H. "Columbus O'Donnell Iselin: 1904–1971." *Biographical Memoirs of the National Academy of Sciences* 64 (1994): 164-187.

–. *Science of the Seven Seas*. New York: Cornell Maritime Press, 1945.

–. "The Westward Intensification of Wind-Driven Ocean Currents." *EOS: Transactions of the American Geophysical Union* 29 (1948): 202-206.

–. "Why We Are Oceanographers." *Oceanography: The Official Magazine of the Oceanography Society* 2, no. 2 (1989): 48-54.

Sullivan, W. "Henry Stommel, 71, Theoretician Influential in Ocean Current Study." *New York Times,* January 21, 1992.

Sunday Times (London). "Under the Sea: An Unexplored World." March 28, 1953.

Sverdrup, H.U., M.W. Johnson, and R.H. Fleming. *The Oceans: Their Physics, Chemistry, and General Biology.* Englewood Cliffs, NJ: Prentice-Hall, 1942.

Teeple, N. "A Brief History of Intrusions into the Canadian Arctic." *Canadian Army Journal* 12.3 (2010): 45-68.

Time. "Sport: Poet of the Depths." March 28, 1960.

Tomaszeski, S.J. "Naval Transformation and the Oceanography Community." *Sea Technology* (January 2004).

Trees, C., V. Sanjuan Calzado, and S. Besiktepe. "Improving Optics–Physics–Biology Coupling in Ocean Ecosystem Models." *EOS: Transactions of the American Geophysical Union* 91, no. 16 (2010): 144.

UN Atlas of the Oceans. January 1, 2000. http://www.oceansatlas.org/servlet/CDSServlet?status=ND0xODc3JjY9ZW4mMzM9KiYzNz1rb3M~.

Under the Cat: Web Site for HMCS Bonaventure. 2001. http://www.underthecat.com/.

United Nations Environment Programme. *Global Programme of Action for the Protection of the Marine Environment from Land Based Activities.* (2011). http://www.gpa.unep.org/.

U.S. Commission on Ocean Policy. *An Ocean Blueprint for the 21ˢᵗ Century.* Final Report. Washington DC, 2004.

Venkataraman, B. "Finding Order in the Apparent Chaos of Currents." *New York Times,* September 28, 2009.

Walker, N.D., A. Haag, S. Balasubramanian, R. Leben, I. Van Heerden, P. Kemp, and H. Mashriqui. "Hurricane Prediction: A Century of Advances." *Oceanography: The Official Magazine of the Oceanography Society* (June 2006).

Washington Post. "CIA Studies Sub Vulnerability." June 6, 1985.

–. "Satellite Part Failure Laid to Complacency in Testing." January 20, 1979.

–. "Shuttle Flight Yields Data on Hiding Subs." March 22, 1985.

–. "Soviets Reportedly Step Up Research to Detect U.S. Subs." September 24, 1986.

Wenk, E. Jr. *The Politics of the Ocean.* Seattle: University of Washington Press, 1972.

Werner, D. "Enhanced NOAA Warning System Provided Detailed Data About Japanese Tsunami." *Space News International (VA)*, April 4, 2011.

–. "Satellites Aiding Disaster Recovery Efforts in Japan." *Space News International (VA)*, March 21, 2011.

Whitehouse, B.G. "The Partitioning of Polynuclear Aromatic Hydrocarbons into the Dissolved Phase of the Aquatic Environment." PhD dissertation. Department of Oceanography, Dalhousie University (NS), 1983.

– and D. Hutt. "Ocean Intelligence in the Maritime Battlespace: The Role of Spaceborne Sensors and HF Radars." *Canadian Military Journal* 5, no. 1 (2004): 35-42.

–, P.W. Vachon, A.C. Thomas, R.J. Quinn, and W.M. Renaud. "Rapid Environmental Assessment (REA) of the Maritime Battlespace." *Canadian Military Journal* 7, no. 1 (2006): 66-68.

Wilcocks, P. "A Chance to Sail the Salish Sea." *Victoria (BC) Times Colonist*, November 5, A10, 2009.

Wunsch, C. "Henry Stommel: September 27, 1920 – January 17, 1992." *Biographical Memoirs of the National Academy of Sciences*. Washington DC: National Academies Press. 1997. http://www.nap.edu/readingroom/books/biomems/hstommel.html.

Yelaja, P. "Royal military renaming slammed as colonial throwback," *CBC website,* August 17, 2011 (www.cbc.ca).

Yoder, J.A., ed. *Status and Plans for Satellite Ocean-Colour Missions: Considerations for Complementary Missions*. Reports of the International Ocean-Colour Coordinating Group, no. 2. Dartmouth (NS), 1999.

–, W.E. Esaias, G.C. Feldman, and C.R. McClain. "Satellite Ocean Color: Status Report." *Oceanography: The Official Magazine of the Oceanography Society,* 1, no. 1 (1988).

– and M.A. Kennelly. "What Have We Learned About Ocean Variability from Satellite Ocean Color Imagers?" *Oceanography: The Official Magazine of the Oceanography Society* (March 2006).

Index

Canadian Forces Reorganization
Act, 181
Canadian Navy, 179, 181
Carson, Rachel, 3-5, 39-40, 89,
122-136, 149-153, 167, 197-
200
Casino Royal, 166
Catworth, 172-173, 195
CCGS *Hudson*, 202
Chatham, 119-120
chemicals, 39
China, 65, 97, 127, 162
chlorinated hydrocarbon, 131
classified view, 92
climate change, 98-99
coast guard, 32
coastal pollution, 42
coastal zone, 6
Coastal Zone Color Scanner, 48,
101
CODAR SeaSondes®, 32
cold-core ring, 29
Cold War, 70, 80, 84-85, 87, 91,
98, 122, 128
colloids, 40
color absorption, 67
color at depth, 66-68, 97

color data, 46-48
color wavelength, 66-67
colors, 67
Commeinhes, Georges, 144
commerce, 49
compressed air diving, 69
Cousteau, Daniel, 138-140
Cousteau, Jacques, 2, 48-49, 53-
55, 67-69, 80, 137-157, 168-
169, 198-200
Cousteau, Simone, 137, 140-142
covert ocean monitoring, 100
currents, 31-32, 51, 72
Curtain, Thomas, 37

data imagery, 46-47
Day After Tomorrow, The, 19, 22
DDT, 131, 133, 136
deep-sea currents, 72
diver support, 56
Doppler radar, 24
Dr. No, 167, 174
Dugan, James, 147-148, 154
Dumas, Frédéric, 139, 141, 143
Durgin, Cyrus, 130
dynamical meteorology, 73
dynamical oceanography, 72-73

dynamics, 7, 71, 90, 122

Earth-observing satellite, 37, 41
Earth-orbiting satellite, 79
echo boomer, 1
ecosystem, 5, 95, 122-123, 136
eddies, 90
Edge of the Sea, The, 125
El Niño, 51
electromagnetic spectrum, 45, 64
energy spectrum, 45
environmental management, 95
environmental models, 37
environmental processes, 14, 27,
   44
environmental sensors, 19
Esquimalt, BC, 107, 110-111,
   191, 207
European Space Agency, 101
eutrophication, 43
Ewing, Maurice, 76

Fessenden oscillator, 152
Fessenden, R.A., 152
Fleming, Ian, 25, 56, 158-170,
   198, 201
Flipper, 174

floats, 21
flooding, 51
France, 16-17
free diving, 145-146
freshwater, 21
Freuchen, Peter, 2-3
Fye, Paul, 76

Gagnan, Émile, 141-144
geostationary satellite, 60
global-ocean-observing system,
   37
global warming, 44
Goci, 60, 62
Godfrey, John, 159
Grand Banks, 36
green, 134
green-house gases, 44
groundwater, 39
Gulf Stream, 28-30, 36, 47

Halifax, NS, 83, 110
Halifax Squadron, 176-177
Helland-Hansen, Bjørn, 74
Hellyer, Paul, 181-183
herbicides, 128, 131
HICO sensor, 64-65

HMCS *Bonaventure (Bonnie)*,
   179-182
HMS *Amethyst*, 161-163
HMS *Consort*, 162
HMS *London*, 161-163
Holbrook, UK, 119
Holdren, John, 95
household chemicals, 39-40
Hudson, Quebec, 135
human activities, 43
Hunt for Red October, The, 90
Hunt, Frederick, 8, 122, 154, 198
Hurricane Juan, 18
Hurricane Katrina, 17
hurricanes, 17-18, 31
hydrocarbons, 42
hydrophone listening device, 152
hydrosphere, 43
hyperspectral sensor, 64, 68

icebergs, 50
infrared energy, 45
infrared region, 64
insecticides, 128, 131
internal waves, 102-103
International Convention for the
   Safety of Life at Sea

(SOLAS), 74
International Hydrographic
   Organization, 4
International Ice Patrol, 74
Intrepid, 165
Iselin, Columbus, 73-76

James Bond, 161, 163-167
Jaws, 176
John C. Stennis Space Flight
   Center, 46

Kipling, Rudyard, 2

Labrador Current, 29, 73
Labrador Sea, 36, 47
Lamont-Doherty Earth
   Observatory, 76
Lamont Geological Observatory,
   76
Landsat, 41, 48
large-scale currents, 51
Le Monde du Silence, 155
Life, 147
littoral zone, 57
Live and Let Die, 169
Living Sea, The, 146

luminescence, 62

MacKay, Peter, 183

macrophytes, 42

Madsen, Axel, 48, 145, 199

mapping, 63

marine acoustic technology, 151

marine acoustics, 75-76, 80, 152

marine biologists, 157

marine biologist's view, 93

marine biology, 84

marine geophysicists, 90

marine model, 25

marine plants, 42, 44

Marine Sciences Council, 202

marine toxicity, 65

marine transportation industry, 36

maritime search and rescue, 31-32

Matsen, Brad, 143

McKinley, Galen, 99

McLean, Scott, 28

Melchior, Simone, 140

mesoscale, 17

mesoscale eddies, 90

messenger, 116

meteorologist, 14

meteorology, 13-16

microwave energy, 45-47

microwave satellite sensors, 50

microwave sensor, 28, 45-48

Mikhail Lomonosov, 86

Mills, Eric L., 72-73, 82

mine countermeasures, 57-58, 79

mine hunting, 58

Mitchell, Joni, 133

modeling, 25

Mohn, Henrik, 72

moonlight, 62

Munk, Walter, 77, 91, 98

Munson, Richard, 49, 144

NASA, 28, 101-102

National Academy of Science's Committee on Oceanography, 87

national defense, 87

National Geographic Society, 4, 154

NATO, 56-57, 79

NATO Undersea Research Center, 96

naval supremacy, 71-72, 98

Neptune Canada program, 28

Nimbus-7, 28

Nixon, Richard, 15, 84

Nova Scotia, 18

nutrient-related activity, 43

*Ocean Blueprint for the 21ˢᵗ
Century, An*, 95

ocean color, 97

ocean-color sensor, 59-60, 64,
102

ocean forecasting, 15

ocean intelligence, 16, 58, 82, 98,
170

ocean-observing satellite, 28

ocean-observing sensors, 46

ocean-observing system, 24, 27,
30-32, 36, 44

ocean weather forecasting, 16

oceanographer, 14, 16

Oceanographer of the US Navy,
57

oceanographic knowledge, 128

oceanography, 1, 7, 125-127, 153,
185

oceanography, pre-WWII, 70

Oceanography Society, 58, 91

oceans, 3-4

Oceans Act of 2000, 95-96

Oceans, The, 82

offshore buoys, 19

offshore oil and gas, 36

operational environmental
information, 57

Operational Line Scanner
sensors, 62

operational oceanography, 14, 16,
56, 58

optical energy, 67

optical oceanography, 58

optical spaceborne sensor, 37

Orion, 191-192

Oshawa, ON, 165

PCBs, 131, 133

pesticides, 40, 129, 135-136

physical oceanographer, 90

physical oceanography, 81

phytoplankton, 42, 45, 47, 55, 63-
65

phytoplankton luminescence, 62

plate tectonics, 90

platforms, 26-27, 59

polar-orbiting satellite, 60

Polaris submarine, 77

CPSIA information can be obtained at www.ICGtesting.com
Printed in the USA
LVOW121422111211

258891LV00006B/3/P